AN HISTORICAL SURVEY OF THE
MIDLAND IN GLOUCESTERSHIRE
Station Layouts and Illustrations

Stonehouse Viaduct
Stonehouse Viaduct, when newly rebuilt in 1884. Sadly, they did not think to photograph the original structure before demolishing it!

National Railway Museum

AN HISTORICAL SURVEY OF THE
MIDLAND IN GLOUCESTERSHIRE
Station Layouts and Illustrations

Peter Smith

Oxford Publishing Company

ISBN 0-86093-301-6

Typesetting by:
Aquarius Typesetting Services, New Milton, Hants.

Printed in Great Britain by:
Biddles Ltd., Guildford, Surrey.

Published by:
Oxford Publishing Co.
Link House
West Street
POOLE, Dorset

Magazine Articles Relating to the Midland Railway in Gloucestershire

Model Railway News, Feb. 1957	Stonehouse and Nailsworth and Dursley branches
Model Railways, Sept. 1979	Nailsworth Station building
Model Railways, April 1973	Wagon turntables, applicable to B&GR stations
Railway Modeller, 1968 (date uncertain)	Yate footbridge (with station photographs)
Railway Modeller, June to Oct. 1971	Midland signalling (includes photograph at Coaley Junction)
Model Railway Constructor, Jan/Feb/Mar. 1980	B&GR wooden bridges
Model Railway Constructor, Nov/Dec. 1979	Private Owner Wagons of Gloucestershire
Model Railways, Jan. 1980	19th century Private Owner Wagons
HMRS Journal, April to June 1983	Gloucester Wagon Co.
Railway World, June 1973	Gloucester stations

BIBLIOGRAPHY

This is a selective Bibliography, as slight reference to these lines are found in many books. It will be seen that relatively little has been published about the area. A list of relevant articles is included separately.

The Bristol & Gloucester Railway by C. Maggs (Oakwood Press) No. 26
The Cheltenham & Gloucester Railway by D. E. Bick (Oakwood Press) No. 43
The Dursley Branch by P. J. Smith (Oakwood Press) No. 131
Regional History of the Railways of Great Britain, Vol. 13 — Thames & Severn by R. Christiansen (David & Charles)
The Severn & Wye Railway by H. W. Paar (David & Charles)
Steam in the West Midlands & Wales by B. J. Ashworth (Ian Allan)
Rail Centre, Bristol by C. Maggs (Ian Allen)
Railway History in Pictures — Wessex by H. C. Casserley (David & Charles)
Private Owner Wagons from The Gloucester Railway Carriage & Wagon Company Ltd. by K. Montague (OPC)
A Pictorial Record of LMS Architecture by V. R. Anderson & G. K. Fox (OPC)
LMS Branch Lines by C. Gammell (OPC)
LMS Engine Sheds (Vol. 2) The Midland Railway by C. Hawkins & G. Reeve (Wild Swan)
LMS General Appendix to Working Timetables (1947) by P. H. Abell (published by author)
Track Layout Diagrams of the GWR & BR (W) — South Gloucestershire & Cheltenham & Gloucester by R. A. Cooke
Sharpness, The Country Dock by W. Rowles (Baileys Ltd., Dursley)
History of Gloucester Docks by M. Stimpson (W. London Industrial Archaeological Society)
Gloucester As It Was (Hendon)
Stroud As It Was (Hendon)
Transport in the Cotswolds by D. J. Viner (Hendon)
An Historical Survey of the Forest of Dean Railways by Peter Smith (OPC)

It must be noted that some of the above titles contain only slight references to the Midland Railway in Gloucestershire, although all are of value.

INTRODUCTION

Had it not been for a remarkable coincidence, the Midland Railway would never have reached Gloucestershire at all. The Birmingham & Gloucester and Bristol & Gloucester companies were independent, and ripe for take-over by the expanding GWR. However, the deal being offered by the GWR was not sufficiently attractive to the Directors of the two companies which by 1845 had combined to form the Bristol & Birmingham Railway. A further meeting was arranged at Paddington, and the Directors' representatives, Edward Sturge and Joseph Gibbons, travelled up to London from Birmingham. By a remarkable coincidence, travelling in the same compartment was John Ellis, Deputy Chairman of the newly-formed Midland Railway and on the journey the three men naturally discussed their reasons for going to London.

By the time the train reached London, it had been agreed that if no agreement could be reached with the GWR, the line would be leased by the Midland Railway, Ellis pledging the Company to the take-over without consulting his Chairman or Board; a very bold step. The GWR would not offer more than it had before, and no agreement was reached, so the GWR, knowing nothing of the arrangement with Ellis, let the line slip through its fingers. The official agreement with the MR came on 30th January 1845, and the GWR found itself sharing its Bristol & Gloucester railway stations with one of its greatest enemies and, even worse, a standard gauge line. The broad gauge monopoly in the Bristol area was broken when the MR line was narrowed in 1854, the Midland Railway having taken over the two lines through the Midland Amalgamation Act of 3rd August 1846.

So it was that the Midland Railway gained access to the south-west of England, the first of many expansions outside the company's original territory, which would lead eventually to Derby-built engines reaching Bournemouth. The line became one of the most important on the system away from the London to Carlisle trunk route and a number of branches were built in the mid-1800s, feeding traffic on to the line. These have now closed, in most cases, but the main line remains busy, having been up-rated for the running of 125m.p.h. trains. John Ellis' shrewd opportunism and bold decisiveness was to pay his employers and their successors a considerable dividend over the ensuing 140 years.

I have tried in this book to give as complete a coverage as possible to the section of the Midland Railway between Mangotsfield, in the south, to Gloucester in the north. The Birmingham & Gloucester line deserves a book in its own right while, to the south, the main line is best considered with the City of Bristol, the Bath line again being excluded as an entity best treated in its own right. Within these parameters, there was a great deal to interest the historian and, I hope, inspire the modeller.

Peter Smith
1985

ACKNOWLEDGEMENTS

This book could never have been written without the generous assistance of many people, foremost among them being Brian Edwards, Colin Maggs and The Revd W. Awdry. I would also like to thank the following people and organisations: Kelvin White, Lens of Sutton, L&GRP, Real Photographs, R. Blencowe, B. J. Ashworth, F. Shuttleworth, H. C. Casserley, D. Ibbotson, the staff of the Gloucester Records Office & Library, the Public Record Office, the HMRS, the National Railway Museum, G. Robinson, H. Ballantyne, P. Copeland, Dr A. Dickens, Cattybrook Brick Co., R. Toop, M. Mensing and D. Cross.

Any extra information on the lines covered would be very much appreciated, particularly as regards the various 'goods only' branches, which seem to have escaped the camera. Any information collected would be made public by way of the MR Society and the HMRS.

Notes on the Author

I am a teacher at a village school in Leicestershire, but I was brought up within sound of the main line between Coaley and Berkeley Road junctions. I have a life-long interest in railways, but am too young to have known much of the age of steam in Gloucestershire. This is my third book on lines in the area, these having stemmed from research done originally because so little had been published about the area. A keen modeller, I have been seduced by the delights of the Great Eastern Railway in Scalefour, although I would love to have the space to model Dudbridge Junction in the 19th century. I am a member of the HMRS, and the GER, MR, and Scalefour societies.

CHRONOLOGY 1: EXCLUDING GLOUCESTER

6th August 1835	Bristol & Gloucestershire Railway opened; Coalpit Heath to Avon Wharf, Bristol.
6th July 1844	Bristol & Gloucester Railway; official opening.
8th July 1844	Bristol & Gloucester Railway; public opening.
7th May 1845	MR takes over the running of the Bristol to Birmingham line.
22nd May 1854	New line opened from Gloucester to Standish, and standard gauge opened to Bristol; Haresfield Station opened.
13th September 1856	Dursley & Midland Junction Railway opened.
1st February 1867	Stonehouse & Nailsworth Railway opened.
26th May 1872	Broad gauge rail removed on the main line and on GWR lines.
2nd September 1872	Yate to Thornbury branch opened.
27th January 1873	Standish Junction reopened; GW running powers to Yate.
2nd August 1875	Sharpness line opened; passenger trains began, August 1876.
16th November 1885	Stroud branch opened to goods; to passengers on 2nd July 1886.
1903	GW goods traffic from new Birmingham line begins to use Standish to Bristol section.
9th March 1908	Yate South Junction opened by GWR, on to new South Wales line. Berkeley Loop also opened and GWR passenger trains began to use main line from Standish to Yate.
1st July 1916	Gossington Sidings and Depot opened.
30th March 1917	Frampton to Frocester line opened.
12th May 1916	Quedgely shell filling factory opened.
27th April 1924	Frocester line closed.
21st February 1926	Gossington Sidings removed (closed 1924).
19th June 1944	Thornbury branch closed to passengers.
8th June 1949	Nailsworth branch; passenger closure made official.
11th December 1961	Frocester Station closed.
10th September 1962	Dursley branch closed to passengers.
January 1963	Berkeley Loop closed.
4th January 1965	Yate, Wickwar, Charfield, Berkeley Road, Coaley, Stonehouse and Haresfield closed.
7th March 1966	Mangotsfield and Bath line closed to passengers.
1st June 1966	Nailsworth and Stroud lines closed.
3rd September 1967	Thornbury branch closed.
1968	Multiple aspect signalling introduced.
18th January 1970	Main line closed south of Yate South Junction.
13th July 1970	Dursley branch closed.
3rd July 1972	Thornbury line reopened to Grovesend Quarry.

CHRONOLOGY 2: GLOUCESTER

1810/11	Cheltenham & Gloucester Railway opened to Gloucester Docks.
1839	Land bought for Birmingham & Gloucester Railway station near the cattle market.
4th November 1840	Birmingham & Gloucester Railway opened.
8th July 1844	Bristol & Gloucester Railway and the C&GWUR opened.
7th May 1845	MR takes over the working of the Bristol to Birmingham line.
1847	GWR Cheltenham Loop and 'T' Station opened.
1848	MR High Orchard dock line opened.
8th July 1850	MR roundhouse locomotive shed opened.
19th September 1851	South Wales Railway opened; all GW trains use SWR station.
22nd May 1854	Tuffley Loop opened, and MR converted to standard gauge.
1861	Cheltenham & Gloucester Railway removed.
26th May 1872	All lines in area became standard gauge, and GW loop lifted.
1895	Barnwood locomotive shed opened.
12th April 1896	New MR station opened.
5th September 1898	MR New Dock line opened from Tuffley Junction.
25th November 1901	GW loop reopened for goods; used for passenger trains from 1st July 1908.
1914	Second platform added to GWR station and new goods shed.
24th May 1938	MR New Dock line closed beyond Hempsted Sidings.
4th May 1964	Barnwood Shed closed.
26th May 1968	New simple layout at Eastgate Station.
14th January 1971	New Dock line closed.
1st October 1971	All MR dock lines closed.
1st December 1975	Eastgate Station and Tuffley Loop closed; new station opened.

CONTENTS

SECTION ONE: GLOUCESTER

THE DEVELOPMENT OF GLOUCESTER'S RAILWAYS

The first railway to serve the City of Gloucester was the standard gauge Birmingham & Gloucester Railway, which approached the city from the north, having passed close to Cheltenham. A pioneer main line, the B&GR opened on 4th November 1840, a terminus station being built on a piece of land near the cattle market. Passenger trains ran from the opening, giving easy access to the Midlands for the first time. However, there was a northern outlet for goods from Gloucester already in existence, the Cheltenham & Gloucester Railway, a 3ft. 6in. gauge plateway which opened during 1810/11. Not a railway in the modern sense, it ran from Cheltenham to Gloucester Docks and, in 1840, the B&GR crossed it on the level, to create Tramway Junction, a name which survives to this day.

The docks had been the main objective of the Birmingham & Gloucester Railway, its station being intended as a temporary structure to be replaced by a station nearer the docks when money was more plentiful. In fact, it was to last until 1896. A rail connection was made with the docks in 1848, but this temporary station determined the site of Gloucester Station right up to the present day.

The Birmingham & Gloucester Railway had received its Act in 1836; in the same year, the Cheltenham & Great Western Union Railway was given powers for a broad gauge line from Cheltenham to Swindon, via Gloucester and Stroud, and the stage was set for the break of gauge that was to become so troublesome. Brunel, the Engineer of the C&GWUR, had his eyes on South Wales, but as money was short, he agreed to share the line of the B&GR from Cheltenham to Gloucester, with a joint Gloucester Station. The Birmingham company sold three acres of land to the north of its station to the C&GWUR for its broad gauge station, which meant that trains from Swindon would have to cross the B&GR on the level at Tramway Junction, where the line to Cheltenham became mixed gauge.

By the time the C&GWUR was ready, the broad gauge Bristol & Gloucester Railway had been built, also by Brunel, joining the C&GWUR at Standish Junction. The two lines opened on 8th July 1844, sharing the broad gauge station. Both lines were expected to become part of the GWR but, in 1845, the Bristol line, together with the line to Birmingham, was taken over by the Midland Railway. With the GWR owning the C&GWUR, not only was there a break of gauge at Gloucester, but two rival companies with a joint station, sharing the main lines to the north and south. The track layout became complicated, with separate goods and locomotive sheds for each gauge, and goods transfer sheds. The convenient arrangement that Brunel envisaged whereby passengers would simply cross a platform from broad to standard gauge trains did not, in practice, work. The facilities provided were very inadequate, as the plans show, and chaos prevailed, so much so that the Gauge Commissioners visited the stations before reporting to Parliament.

The arrangement of two adjacent terminal stations did not last very long, fortunately, as in 1847 the GWR opened the Cheltenham Loop, by which trains could avoid Gloucester altogether, and on this line was built a station called the 'T' Station (from its shape). Here, coaches were dropped off trains to and from Cheltenham, and then run into Gloucester separately. In 1848, a branch was built by the MR to Gloucester Docks, the High Orchard line, which superseded the connection to the tramway put in by the Birmingham & Gloucester Railway. This mixed gauge line diverged from the main line near Tramway Junction.

The next development of importance came on 19th September 1851, when the South Wales Railway, in the guise of the Gloucester & Dean Forest Railway, opened its line from Chepstow. A new station, with two platforms and an overall roof, was built north of the existing stations, the line running through to form an end on connection with the GWR from Swindon and Cheltenham. The GWR at once stopped using the old C&GWUR terminus, which was, from then on, only used by the MR Bristol trains. The Cheltenham Loop and the 'T' Station were abandoned, although tracks remained in place, all GWR trains using the new SWR station. This must have proved inadequate as, in 1855, a larger station was opened on the same site; the original may only have been intended as a temporary structure.

The SWR opened locomotive sheds north of the line near Horton Road Crossing (then called Asylum Lane), this becoming the GWR Horton Road sheds that remained until the end of steam. There were goods sidings between the sheds and the platforms, with a large goods shed east of the station.

Things remained thus for only a short time and on 22nd May 1854, the MR opened its independent standard gauge route to the south, looping round through Gloucester to Tuffley. The MR became entirely standard gauge, and the broad gauge station was closed, the site being used for carriage sidings. All traffic was concentrated at the old Birmingham station, the platforms being lengthened. The old locomotive sheds had been superseded by a standard roundhouse shed, which opened on 8th July 1850, an early example of the standard MR shed of the period. For the first time, the MR and the GWR were largely separate, apart from the shared line to Cheltenham. Midland Railway trains had to reverse at Gloucester, the Tuffley Loop diverging from the station lines near Tramway Junction.

The C&G Tramway closed finally in 1861, and was removed; the railways having taken all its traffic. The course remained as a path, and the name of Tramway Junction ensures that it is remembered.

For the first time since 1840, the railways at Gloucester remained unaltered for a period of several years, until 26th May 1872, when the broad gauge was removed from all the GWR lines in the area. The layout of the goods yard could now be greatly simplified and the MR cleared away all the old sheds and built a large new brick goods shed, which remained in use well into the 1960s. With no need for a transfer shed, there was little connection between the two companies' yards. There followed a further period of stability, until the awkward arrangement of the MR terminus finally became too much to bear. The 'temporary' station of 1840 was not a good advertisement for the Midland Railway, and was attracting much adverse comment locally. On 12th April 1896, a totally new through station was opened on the Tuffley Curve, with long spacious platforms and attractive brick buildings with wide glazed canopies. The old station was closed, becoming more carriage sidings; the roundhouse had already gone, replaced by a new shed on the Barnwood Curve during the previous year. A water tower and turntable were built near the station to avoid light engine movements over Tramway Junction. The High Orchard line was realigned, and only the goods shed and yard remained much the same. All the MR lines in the Gloucester area were resignalled at the same time, having first been equipped with standard slotted post signals in the early 1870s.

The GWR had remained fairly static during this period of change on the MR. However, in 1901, the Cheltenham Loop was relaid, the track bed having been retained after removal of the track in 1872; it was opened again to allow goods trains to pass Gloucester, many running south on to the MR at Standish Junction, using running powers to the south. The new GWR line from Birmingham increased traffic, and the loop was used for passenger trains from 9th March 1908, these running on to the new GWR line at Yate. The new Wolverhampton to Bristol expresses were the first to regularly use the line.

In 1914, the GWR station was extended with a new platform north of the running lines, a new goods shed replacing the old SWR building and the station was resignalled.

The next development on the MR came on 5th November 1898, when the New Dock branch was opened from Tuffley Junction, running south-west to Hempsted Sidings, where it crossed the canal to join up with lines on the west of the canal. A connection was made in 1913 to Gloucester gasworks.

So far, all the alterations to the railways at Gloucester had been made to cope with increasing traffic. However, after World War I, there was a period of consolidation, with the Grouping in 1923. Little change was apparent at Gloucester until the late 1930s, other than to rolling stock and locomotives, but in 1938 the New Dock line was cut back to Hempsted Sidings. Not until the 1960s did any serious contraction of the layout take place; indeed, in 1942, the Barnwood Curve and the line to Cheltenham were quadrupled. However, the stimulus given by the war was only temporary, and in the 1960s the goods lines and sidings were progressively less used. The locomotive depot at Barnwood finally closed on 4th May 1964, Horton Road remaining only as a stabling point. In 1968, an automatic signalling scheme was introduced, and most signal boxes in the Gloucester area were closed, only those on the Tuffley Loop remaining to control the level crossings. The former MR station, named Gloucester (Eastgate) by BR, was reduced to two platform faces, and the 1914 platform at Gloucester (Central), the GWR station, was closed. The MR goods yard was taken out of use, all traffic being dealt with in the ex-GWR yards. On 14th January 1971, the Hempsted Dock branch closed, followed by the High Orchard line later the same year, leaving only the GW line from Over Junction to serve the docks.

There had been a number of schemes for a joint station at Gloucester over the years and, in the 1890s, one was suggested near Tramway Junction. In the late 1960s, BR began looking again at such an idea, the favoured site being on the Barnwood Curve, with a single long island platform between the running lines. The plan was rejected because of the distance from the city centre, but a new station was still desirable. BR wished to close the Tuffley Loop and thus remove four of the five level crossings in the city. If the loop closed, so must Eastgate Station, so it was finally decided to build a new station on the site of Gloucester (Central), the old GWR station. The long platform was retained, with brand new buildings and a revised layout. The new station was opened on 1st December 1975, and the MR line was closed. Eastgate was soon demolished and the entire site has now been cleared and redeveloped. North to south trains now have to reverse, just as they did in 1844, but with diesel power this is a relatively quick operation; many trains simply bypass Gloucester altogether. The layout of Gloucester's railways has reverted virtually to that with which it began in the 1840s.

Gloucester has a convenient new station, and an excellent train service, but little remains for the historian. I know of no other place of comparable size that has so totally removed all signs of its railway history. Hardly a building remains from the MR, and only the 1914 platform buildings, in use for parcels, from the GWR. The docks are hardly used. Gloucester has turned its back on its railway past, and we are fortunate that much has survived in the form of plans, maps, and pictures.

Gloucester
A special train, to celebrate the centenary of the Dursley branch in 1956, stands at Gloucester Station.

L&GRP

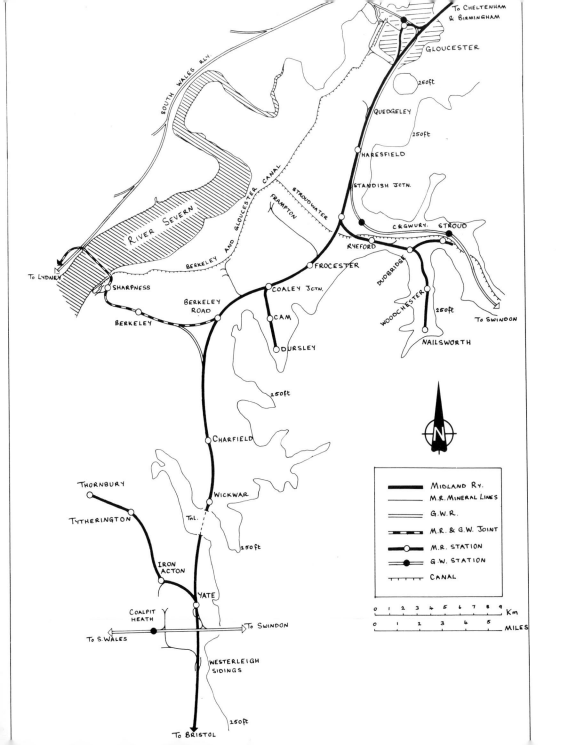

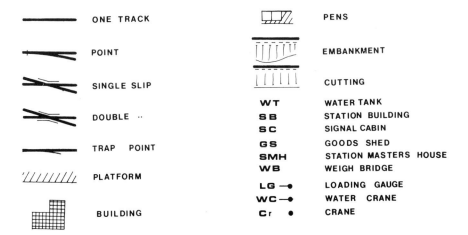

KEY TO MAIN PLANS

———	ONE TRACK		⊞	PENS
	POINT			EMBANKMENT
	SINGLE SLIP			CUTTING
	DOUBLE ..		WT	WATER TANK
	TRAP POINT		S B	STATION BUILDING
/////	PLATFORM		SC	SIGNAL CABIN
	BUILDING		GS	GOODS SHED
			SMH	STATION MASTERS HOUSE
			WB	WEIGH BRIDGE
			LG ●	LOADING GAUGE
			WC ●	WATER CRANE
			Cr ●	CRANE

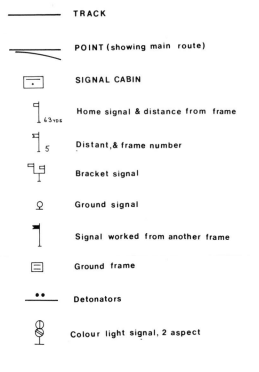

KEY TO SIGNALLING PLANS

- ——— TRACK
- POINT (showing main route)
- SIGNAL CABIN
- Home signal & distance from frame (63 YDS)
- Distant, & frame number (5)
- Bracket signal
- Ground signal
- Signal worked from another frame
- Ground frame
- •• Detonators
- Colour light signal, 2 aspect

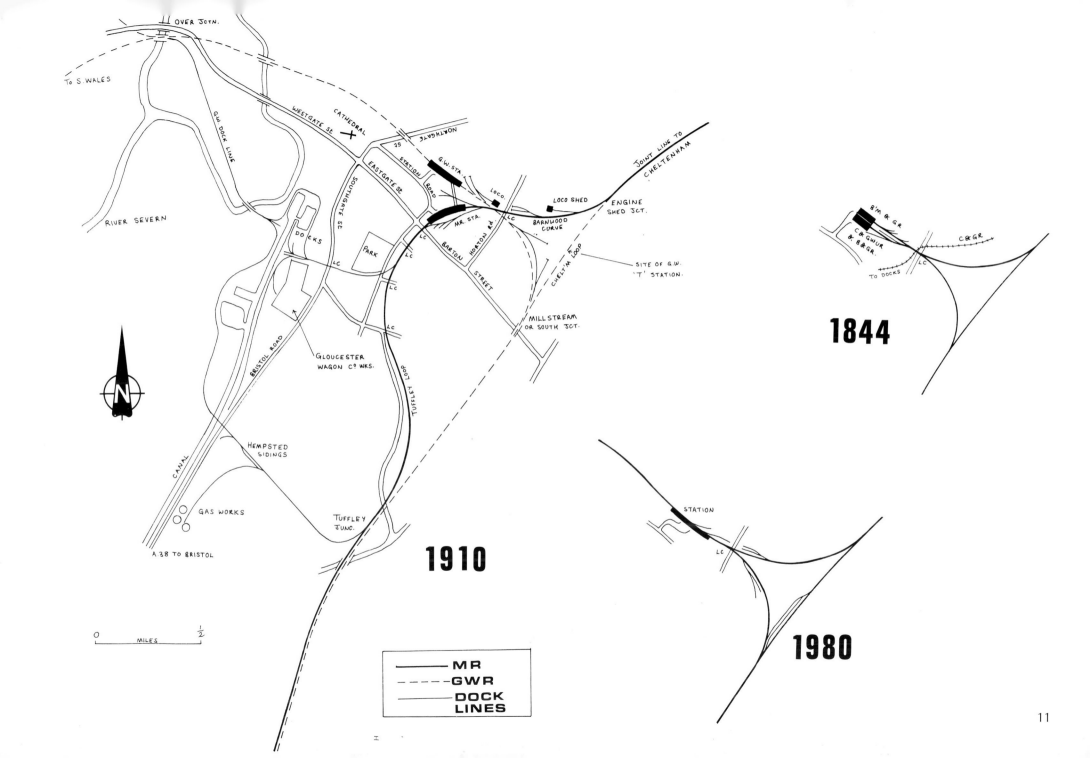

TO S. WALES

OVER JCTN.

GW DOCK LINE

WESTGATE ST.

CATHEDRAL

NORTHGATE ST.

EASTGATE ST.

STATION ROAD

G.W. STA.

LOCO.

LOCO SHED

JOINT LINE TO CHELTENHAM

ENGINE SHED JCT.

RIVER SEVERN

SOUTHGATE ST.

DOCKS

PARK

LC

MR. STA.

HORTON Rd.

LC

BARNWOOD CURVE

BARTON STREET

CHEL'M LOOP

SITE OF G.W. 'T' STATION.

LC

MILL STREAM OR SOUTH JCT.

N

BRISTOL ROAD

GLOUCESTER WAGON C° WKS.

TUFFLEY LOOP

LC

CANAL

HEMPSTED SIDINGS

GAS WORKS

TUFFLEY JUNC.

A.38 TO BRISTOL

0   MILES   ½

1910

B'M & GR

C & GWUR & B & GR.

C & GR

LC

TO DOCKS

1844

STATION

LC

1980

MR
GWR
DOCK LINES

11

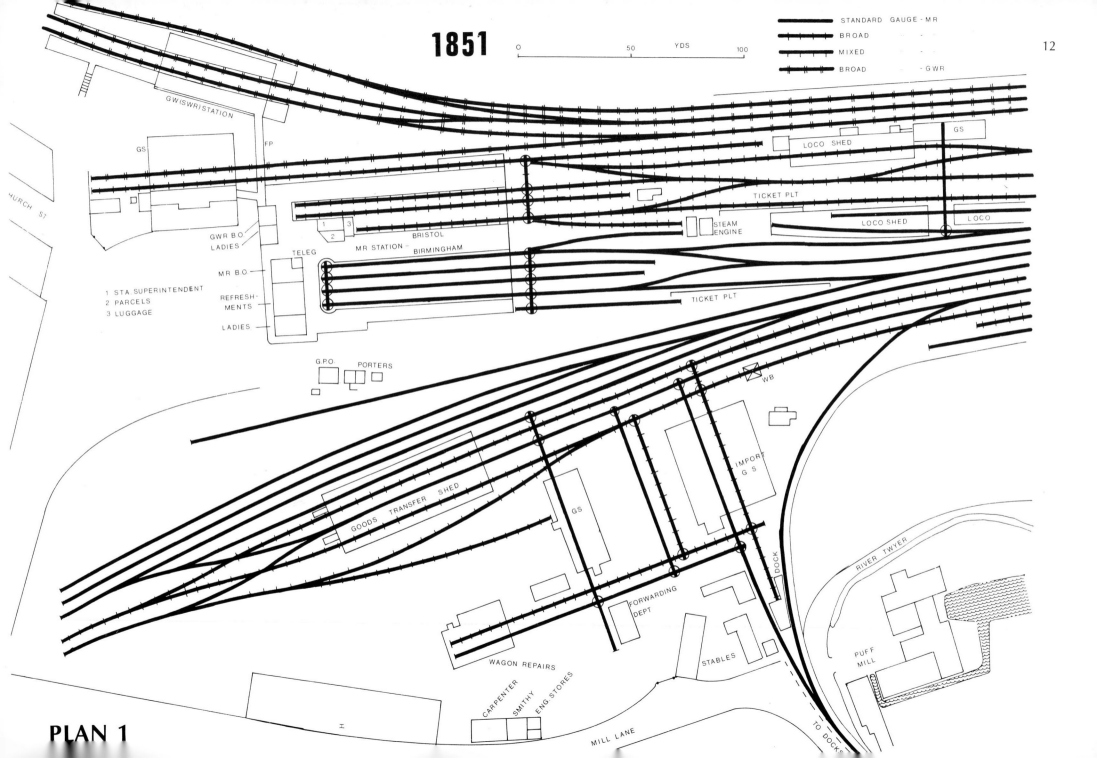

1851

STANDARD GAUGE - MR
BROAD
MIXED
BROAD - GWR

0   50   YDS   100

12

GW (SWR) STATION

CHURCH ST

GS

FP

GWR B.O.
LADIES

MR B.O.

REFRESH-
MENTS

LADIES

TELEG

1 3
2

MR STATION - BRISTOL
BIRMINGHAM

STEAM
ENGINE

TICKET PLT

LOCO SHED

GS

LOCO SHED

LOCO

TICKET PLT

1 STA. SUPERINTENDENT
2 PARCELS
3 LUGGAGE

G.P.O.   PORTERS

WB

IMPORT
G S

GOODS TRANSFER SHED

GS

RIVER TWYER

FORWARDING
DEPT

DOCK

PUFF
MILL

WAGON REPAIRS

STABLES

CARPENTER SMITHY ENG. STORES

MILL LANE

TO DOCKS

PLAN 1

PLAN 1: An enlargement of the station area as it was in 1851, showing the Birmingham & Gloucester Railway's terminus with standard gauge track and to the north, the broad gauge C&GWUR terminus, then used by the MR Bristol trains. Beyond this is the SWR/GWR station, used by all the GWR trains. There is a small broad gauge goods shed near the SWR station, but the main goods yard is south of the MR station in the area known as Wheeler's Nursery. Here there is a large goods transfer shed, served by both broad and standard gauge tracks, and other goods sheds are at right angles to the running lines, fed from turntables. To the south runs the goods only line to the docks, later joining the course of the tramway.

There are small locomotive sheds for both gauges, although the roundhouse had been opened by this time; these are not main depots, those being at Bristol, Swindon and Bromsgrove.

Noteworthy is the wide use of turntables; they were great space savers, and it should be remembered that points were rather crude in those days. Many were stub points of the type now associated with narrow gauge lines, and they were worked from capstans near the blades. The three stations had overall roofs, that over the SWR station being very small. No buildings are shown here, possibly simply because this is a MR plan. A GWR booking office is shown, from which a path leads to the platforms. No access from the north is shown, although a subway runs under the station. In the south-eastern corner of the plan is Puff Mill, a water-powered mill, which was demolished in 1853.

Gloucester
The MR terminus, built by the Birmingham & Gloucester Railway in 1840, seen in the 1880s. The GWR station is on the left.

L&GRP

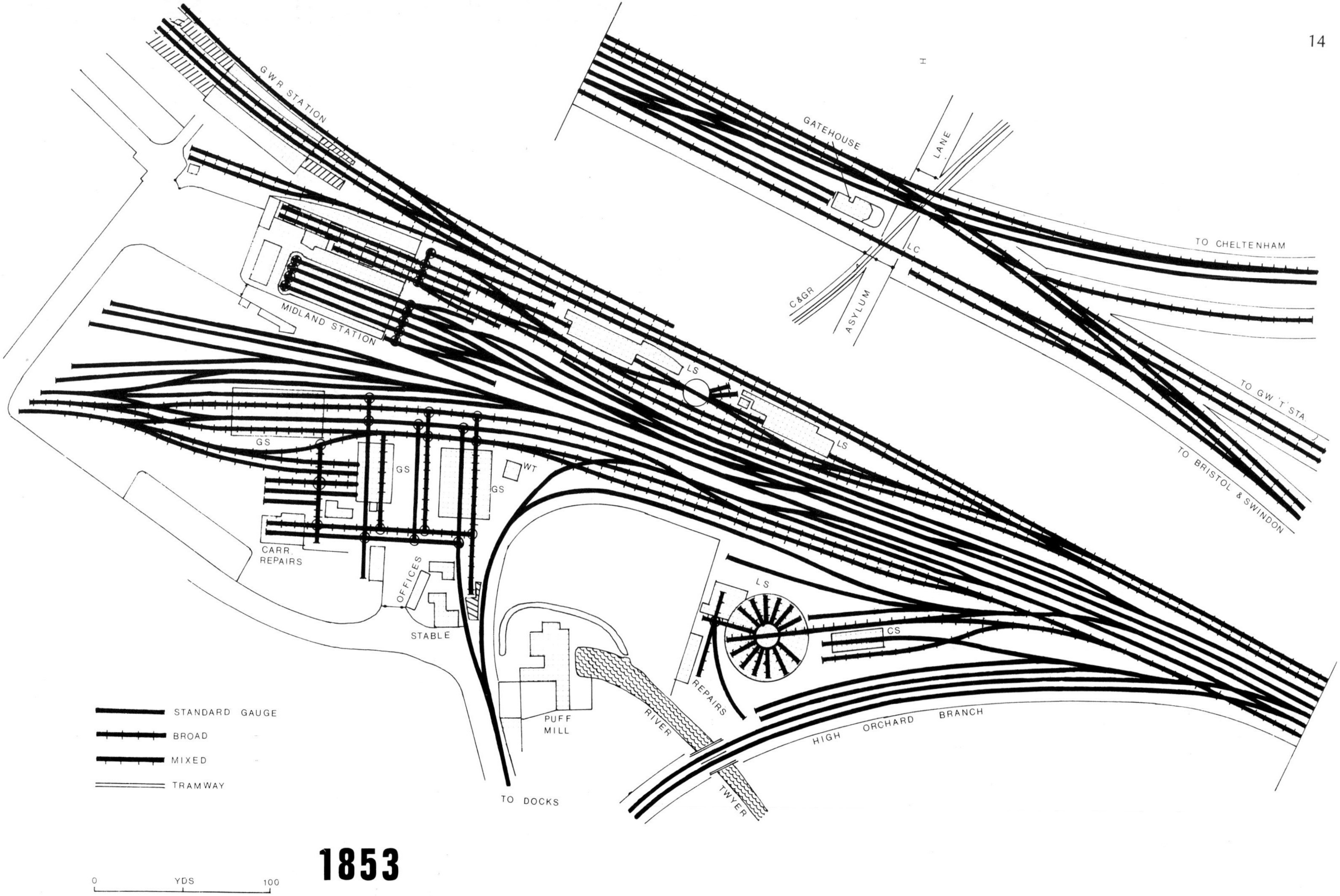

GWR STATION

TO CHELTENHAM

GATEHOUSE

LANE

C & G R

LC

A SYLUM

MIDLAND STATION

TO GW 'T' STA.

LS

LS

LS

TO BRISTOL & SWINDON

GS

GS

WT

GS

CARR.
REPAIRS

OFFICES

STABLE

LS

REPAIRS

CS

PUFF
MILL

RIVER

TWYER

HIGH ORCHARD BRANCH

TO DOCKS

STANDARD GAUGE
BROAD
MIXED
TRAMWAY

0   YDS   100

1853

PLAN 2

PLAN 2: The second plan shows the whole station area in 1853. Taken again from a Midland Railway survey, it again shows none of the GWR sidings, etc. Considerable development has taken place since 1851, but the passenger stations themselves are the same. The standard gauge locomotive sheds have been removed, having been rendered surplus by the roundhouse, which is shown. Opened on 8th July 1850, there are 14 roads around a 39ft. turntable. MR code No. 7, it had a repair shop at the rear, and a separate coke shed. The shed was of mixed gauge until 1854. The building was no doubt similar to the familiar roundhouse at Derby, erected about the same time, being an early example of a standard design.

The broad gauge sheds remain (they were demolished in 1854), and passing south of the roundhouse is seen the High Orchard dock line of 1848, which joins the line running from the goods yard. Extra sidings have been put in here and the small goods shed near the SWR station has gone, although the siding remains.

Tramway Junction can be seen, with the Cheltenham and Bristol/Swindon lines crossing on the level, all of them crossing the tramway, making a very complex piece of trackwork. East of the junction, the GWR line, shared by the MR, turns south, the line to the GW 'T' Station diverging. The standard gauge MR line turns north, soon joined by the GWR to become mixed gauge; the GW line from Cheltenham maintains a separate course. The gatekeeper's house stands between the tracks next to the crossing, the road at that time being called Asylum Lane.

Gloucester

The last train to leave the old terminus, in December 1896, behind 2-4-0 No. 1295. Note the LNWR coaches behind the engine.

L&GRP

Gloucester

GWR 'Bulldog' class locomotive No. 3320 *Avalon* stands at Gloucester Station on 1st May 1926.

H. C. Casserley

Gloucester

A 'Spinner' stands next to platform 1 on a permanent way train, circa 1910.

L&GRP

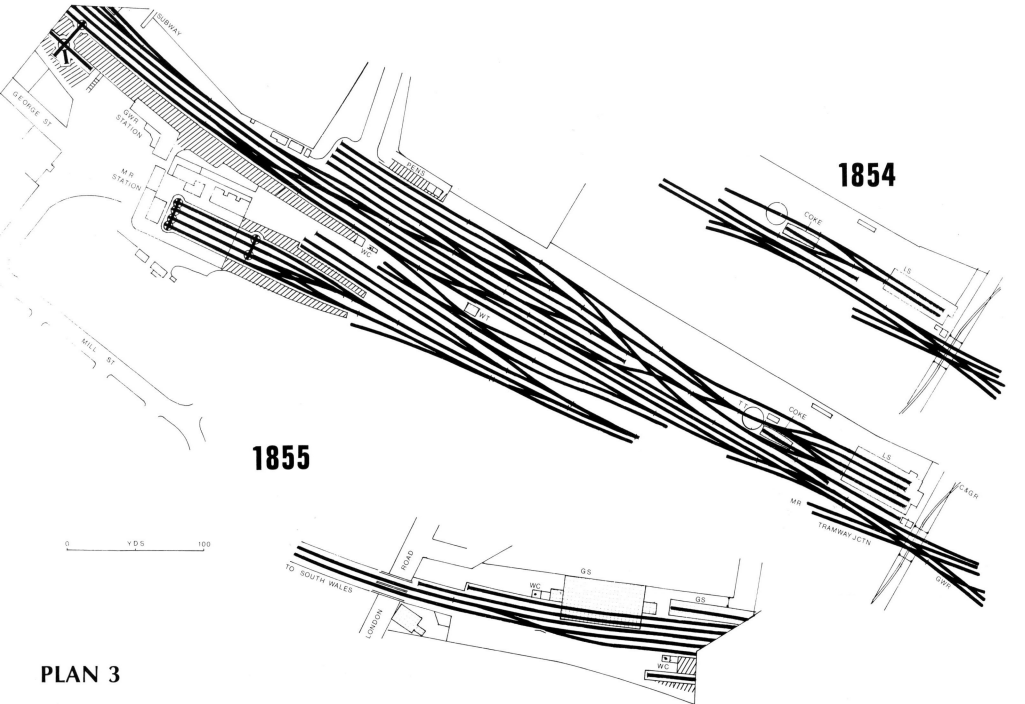

16

SUBWAY

GEORGE ST

GWR STATION

MR STATION

PENS

1854

COKE

LS

WC

WT

MILL ST

1855

TT

COKE

LS

C&GR

0   YDS   100

MR

TRAMWAY JCTN

TO SOUTH WALES

ROAD

GWR

GS

WC

GS

LONDON

WC

PLAN 3

PLAN 3: This plan was taken from a GWR survey, showing the new GWR station in 1855. This was built to replace the old SWR station, and had a 280 yard platform with a double crossover half-way along. Part of the MR station is also shown, of interest because by now all the MR lines are standard gauge, the Tuffley Loop having been built in 1854. The old broad gauge terminus has been closed and removed, the site being carriage sidings. New buildings cover the former platforms. The GWR sidings and goods shed are shown, these no doubt existing from 1851 when the first station opened. Similarly shown are the locomotive sheds, which by 1855 had evolved into a four-road depot; the earlier two road shed is also shown.

Some rather odd track is shown near the MR station; this is no doubt left over from the abolition of the broad gauge on the MR, as it is only connected to the GWR, and may have been in course of alteration when the survey was made. The MR goods yard is not shown, although it was no doubt similar to the layout of 1853, with the deletion of the broad gauge sidings. The transfer shed probably retained broad gauge roads for the transfer of goods to GWR wagons. Unfortunately, no distinction is made between the gauges on the plan on which this is based.

Gloucester
The GWR sheds at Horton Road, Gloucester.

HMRS

Gloucester
Ex-LMS Compound No. 41195 enters Gloucester from the north. Note the MR name boards.
H. C. Casserley

Gloucester
No. 40928 double-heads a northbound train with another Compound on 11th July 1956.
H. C. Casserley

1880

PLAN 4

PLAN 4: This plan shows the station area in 1880, and includes much of the GWR station. There has been considerable development; all lines are now standard gauge, and although the locomotive shed and passenger station are similar to the 1853 arrangement, the goods facilities have been transformed. The goods yard was probably altered in 1872, when the broad gauge was abolished on the GWR. A fan of sidings flanks the Tuffley Loop, serving the docks, and the layout is now fully controlled from signal boxes; this work also dating from the early 1870s.

The GWR Horton Road engine shed has been greatly expanded, but the remainder of the GWR has not changed much; the SWR goods shed remained in use. Puff Mill has gone, demolished to make way for the Tuffley Loop, and the River Twyer was culverted under the whole site. The line of the tramway is seen as a path, running south of the High Orchard Sidings and under the loop line. Asylum Lane has become Horton Road, as it is known today.

An enlargement is provided showing the layout at Tramway Junction, as this is rather complicated, and another enlargement to show the buildings at the MR station.

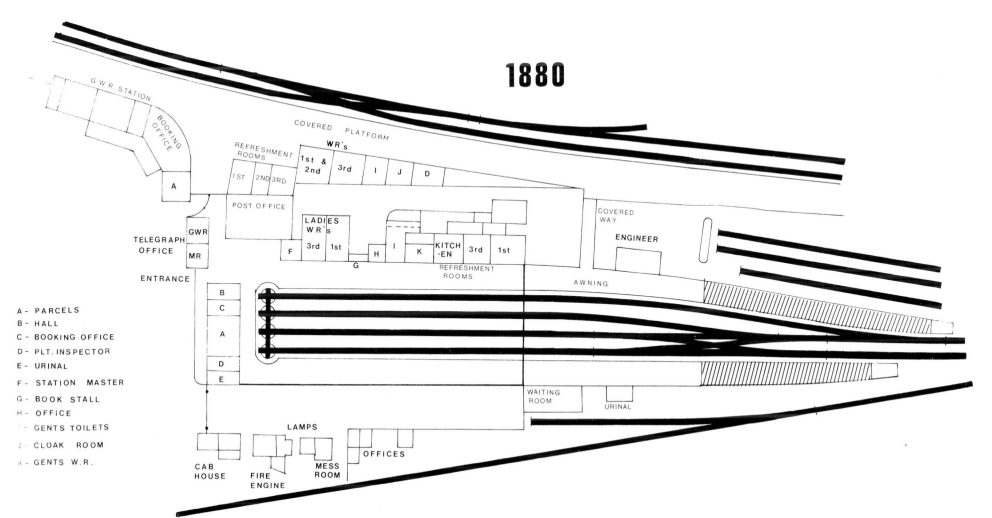

1880

A – PARCELS
B – HALL
C – BOOKING OFFICE
D – PLT. INSPECTOR
E – URINAL
F – STATION MASTER
G – BOOK STALL
H – OFFICE
I – GENTS TOILETS
J – CLOAK ROOM
K – GENTS W.R.

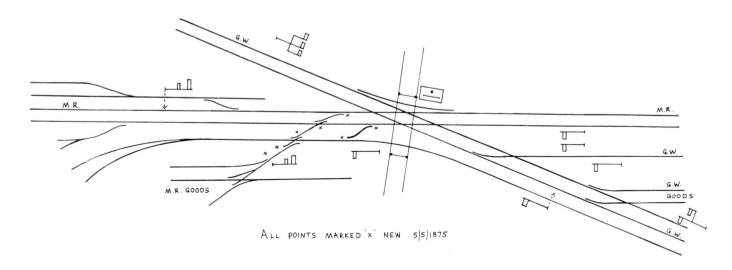

All points marked 'x' new 5/5/1875

TRAMWAY JCTN.

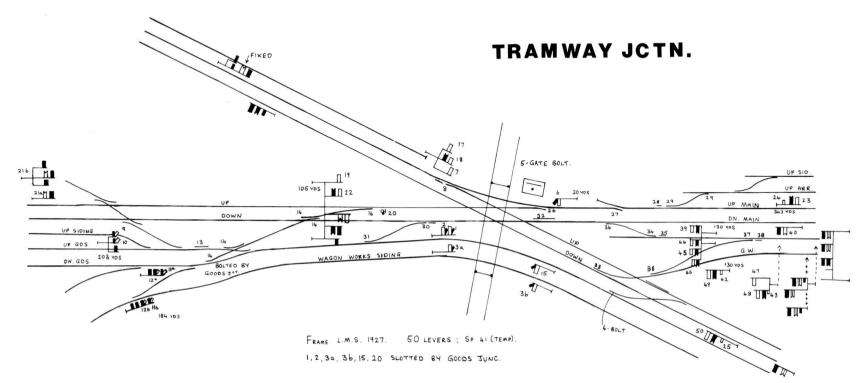

Frame L.M.S. 1927.   50 levers ; Sp 41 (temp).

1, 2, 3a, 3b, 15, 20 slotted by goods junc.

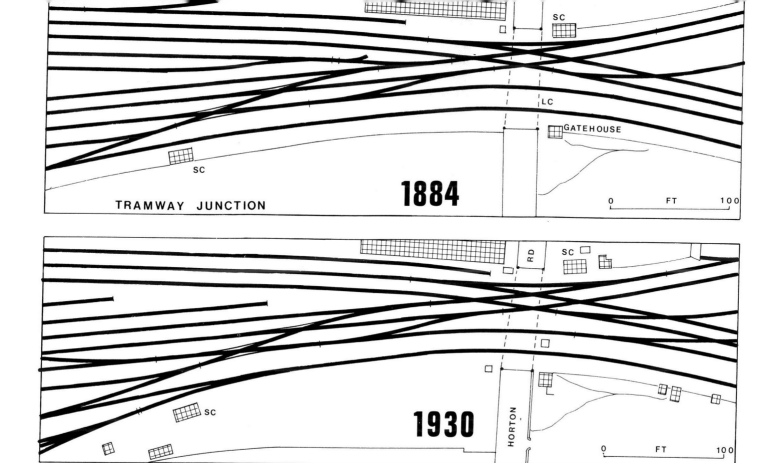

TRAMWAY JUNCTION

1884

LC

GATEHOUSE

SC

0 FT 100

1930

HORTON

RD SC

SC

0 FT 100

Gloucester
Tramway Junction, with 0-6-0PT No. 3693 on a transfer goods, in March 1964.
R. Blencowe

Gloucester
'Hall' class locomotive No. 6956 *Mottram Hall* enters Gloucester past Tramway Junction in June 1964.

R. Blencowe

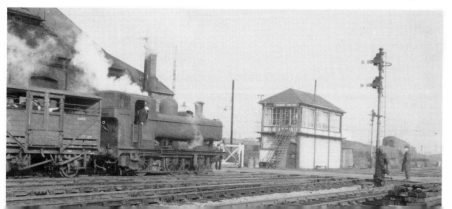

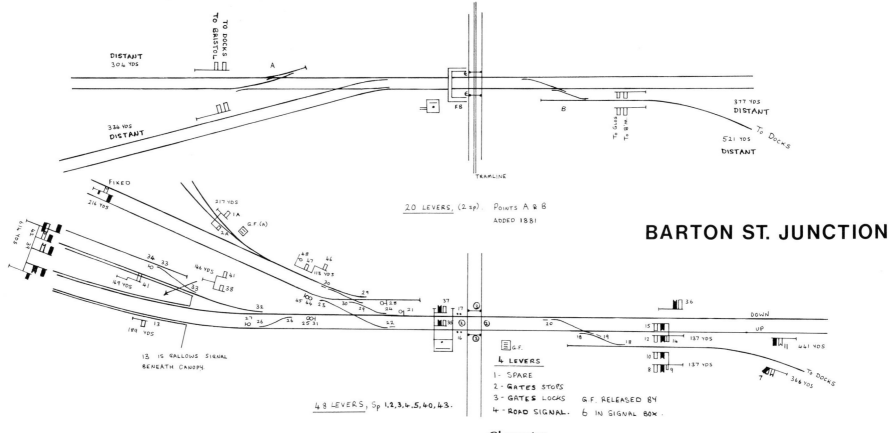

BARTON ST. JUNCTION

DISTANT 304 YDS

TO DOCKS
TO BRISTOL

A

334 YDS DISTANT

216 YDS FIXED

217 YDS

G.F. (A)

20 LEVERS, (2 sp). POINTS A & B
ADDED 1881

TRAMLINE

FB

B

To Glos W.B.
To

377 YDS DISTANT

521 YDS DISTANT

To Docks

13 IS GALLOWS SIGNAL BENEATH CANOPY.

48 LEVERS, Sp 1,2,3,4,5,40,43.

DOWN

UP

To DOCKS

G.F.
4 LEVERS
1 - SPARE
2 - GATES STOPS
3 - GATES LOCKS   G.F. RELEASED 84
4 - ROAD SIGNAL.   6 IN SIGNAL BOX.

137 YDS
461 YDS
366 YDS
137 YDS

Gloucester
Barton Street Junction signal box.

K. White

Gloucester
The rear of Barton Street box.

K. White

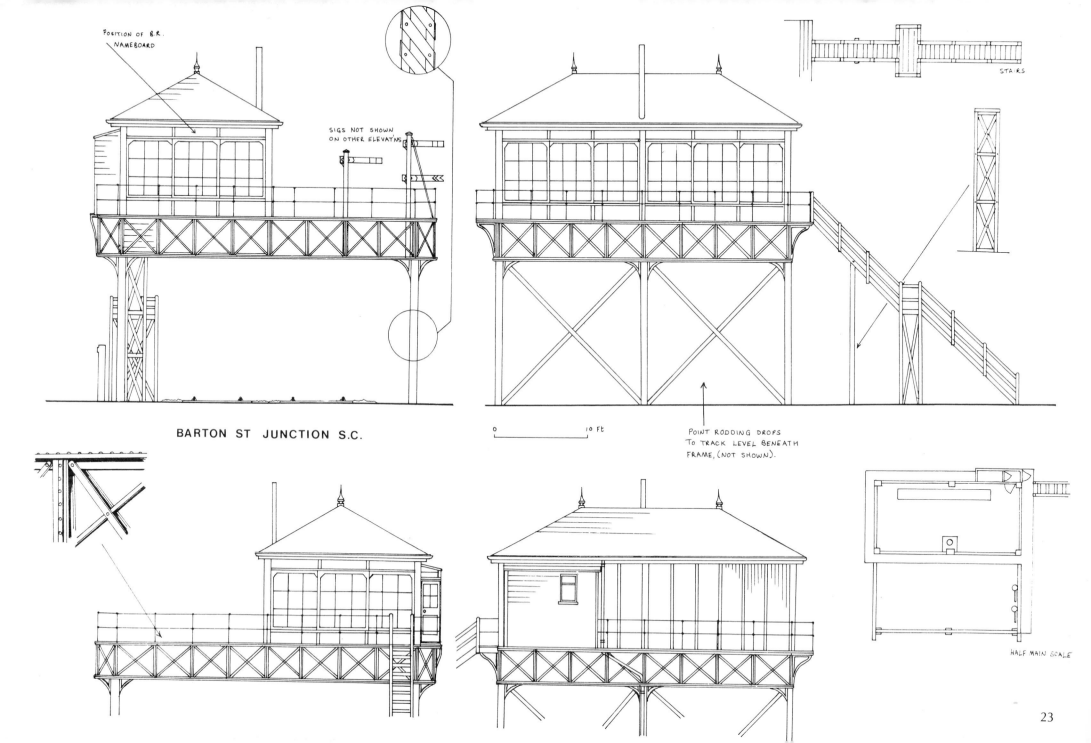

POSITION OF B.R.
NAMEBOARD

SIGS NOT SHOWN
ON OTHER ELEVAT'NS

STAIRS

BARTON ST JUNCTION S.C.

0   10 Ft

POINT RODDING DROPS
TO TRACK LEVEL BENEATH
FRAME, (NOT SHOWN).

HALF MAIN SCALE

23

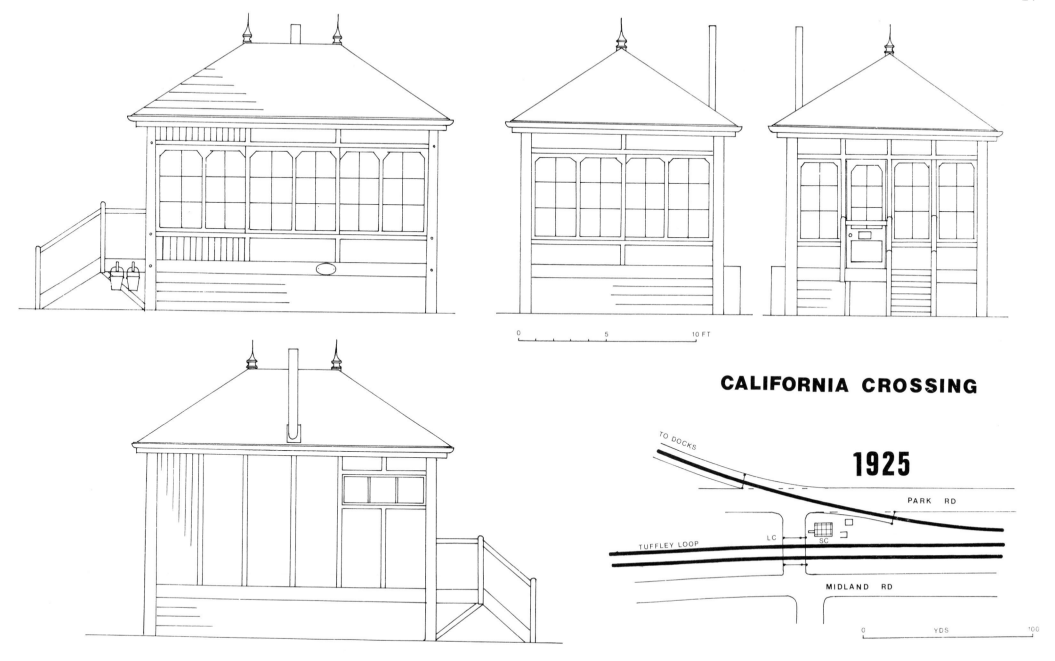

CALIFORNIA CROSSING

1925

TO DOCKS

PARK RD

TUFFLEY LOOP

LC   SC

MIDLAND RD

0   5   10 FT

0   YDS   100

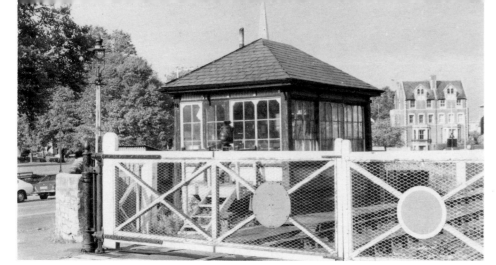

Gloucester
California Crossing, with the signal box.
K. White

PLAN 5: This shows the Tuffley Loop line between Barton Street Junction and the divergence of the dock line at California Crossing. The High Orchard line skirted Gloucester Park before crossing Bristol Road and entering the docks. It became double track about 50yds. beyond the end of the line on the plan. The signals in 1880 were of the MR slotted post type.

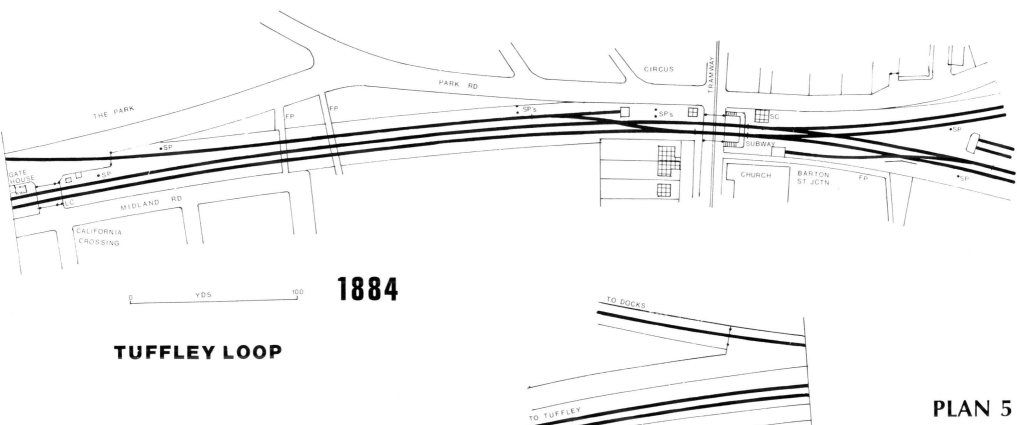

1884

TUFFLEY LOOP

PLAN 5

25

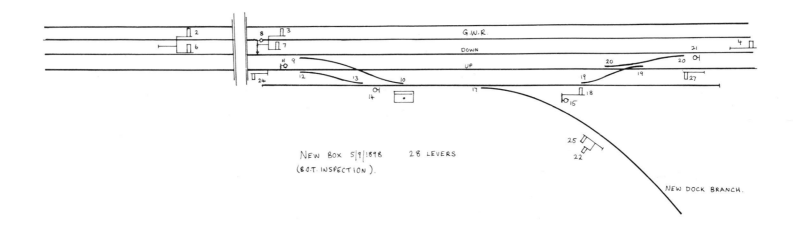

New Box 5/9/1898   28 Levers
(B.O.T. Inspection).

G.W.R.
DOWN
UP

New Dock Branch.

TUFFLEY LOOP

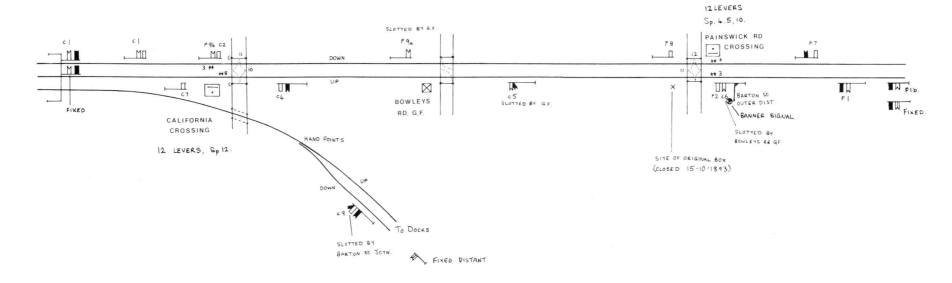

12 Levers
Sp. 4, 5, 10.

PAINSWICK RD
CROSSING

SLOTTED BY G.F.

DOWN
UP

BOWLEYS
RD. G.F.

Barton St
Outer Dist.

BANNER SIGNAL.

SLOTTED BY
Bowleys Rd GF

SLOTTED BY G.F.

FIXED

CALIFORNIA
CROSSING

12 LEVERS, Sp 12.

HAND POINTS

SITE OF ORIGINAL BOX
(CLOSED 15-10-1893)

FIXED.

DOWN
UP

To Docks

SLOTTED BY
Barton St Jctn.

FIXED DISTANT

Gloucester
Tuffley Junction, circa 1920, photographed from the branch.

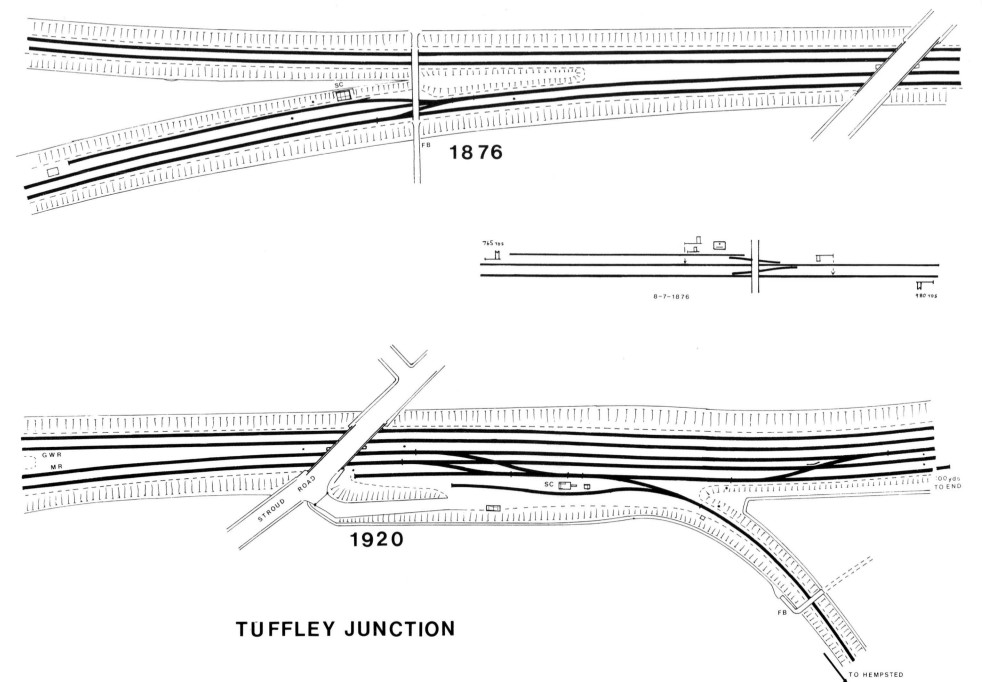

1876

8-7-1876 · 765 yds · 980 yds

1920

GWR
MR

STROUD ROAD

SC

FB

TO HEMPSTED

TUFFLEY JUNCTION

Gloucester
A closer view of Tuffley Junction, circa 1920.

National Railway Museum

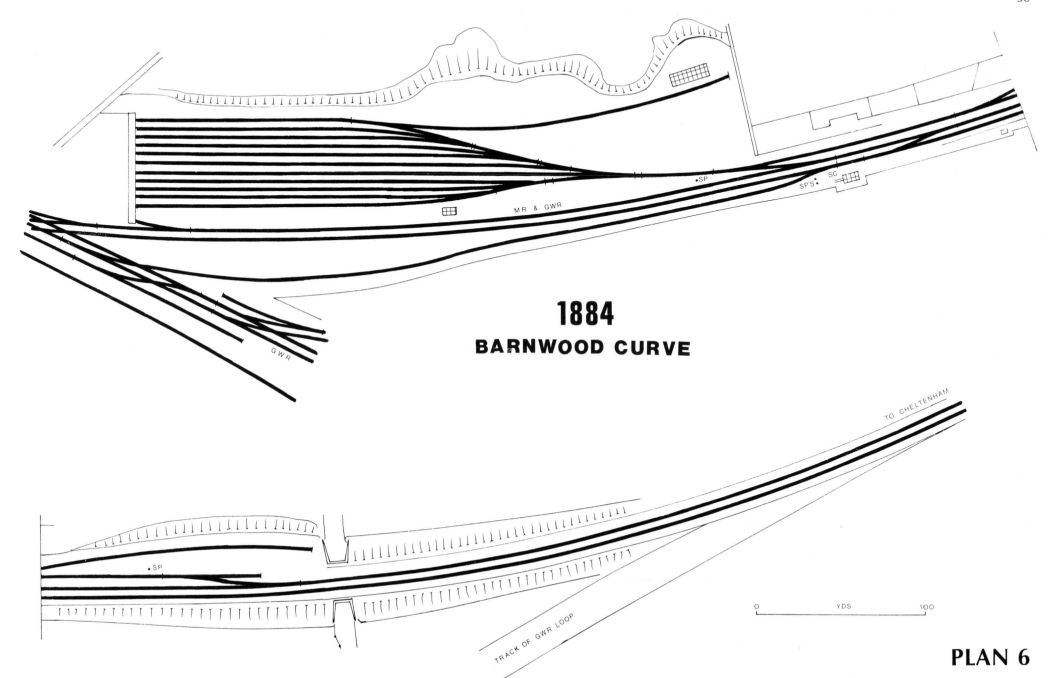

1884

BARNWOOD CURVE

MR & GWR

GWR

SP

SP'S

SC

TO CHELTENHAM

SP

TRACK OF GWR LOOP

O   YDS   100

PLAN 6

PLAN 6: This plan shows the Barnwood Curve in 1880, from Tramway Junction to the trackbed of the GW Cheltenham Loop, lifted in 1872. The sidings shown are all MR property, the section of line from Gloucester to Churchdown being owned by the MR, and used by both companies.

Gloucester
Barnwood Curve, with the engine sheds beyond, circa 1947.

HMRS

Gloucester
No. 9453 brings the 'Cheltenham Spa Express' off Barnwood Curve in March 1964.
R. Blencowe

Gloucester
A view looking across Barnwood Curve, opposite the sidings, circa 1947.

HMRS

G W STATION

CARR. SDGS.

SC

GWR

WT

TATE & LYLE Ltd.

GS

Crs

STATION ROAD

OFFICES

STABLE

MESS ROOM

SC

GW LOCO SHED

SB

FB

HORTON RD.

FP

SC

SC

PLAN 7

SC

WAGON REPAIR SDGS

Cr

FP

0   YDS   100

BARTON

SC

CHURCH

1932

PLAN 7: The station area in 1932, showing the new MR station of 1896. The old terminus has become carriage sidings, and the goods yard has changed little. The roundhouse has gone, being replaced by Barnwood Shed in 1895, and a 190ft. footbridge crosses the yard to connect the two stations. The GWR platform of 1914 can be seen, although most GWR tracks are omitted from the LMS plan on which this is based. In the goods yard, five short sidings beyond the goods shed were hired out to local firms such as coal merchants — modellers will recognise the name of one; Burtt, a beehive manufacturer. Market Street had now become Station Road, the new station giving people a longer walk from the city centre.

Detailed enlargements are provided in this volume covering Tramway Junction, the goods yard (also applicable to 1880), and the platform buildings.

Gloucester
Ex-LMS 'Jubilee' No. 45682 *Hawke* stands at Gloucester, with the water tower and GWR goods shed beyond.

Author's Collection

Gloucester
The site of the terminus in use as carriage sidings in 1939.

L&GRP

Gloucester
Ex-GWR 'Grange', No. 6815 *Frilford Grange*, enters the station in October 1963. On the right is the transfer line to the LMS yard.

R. Blencowe

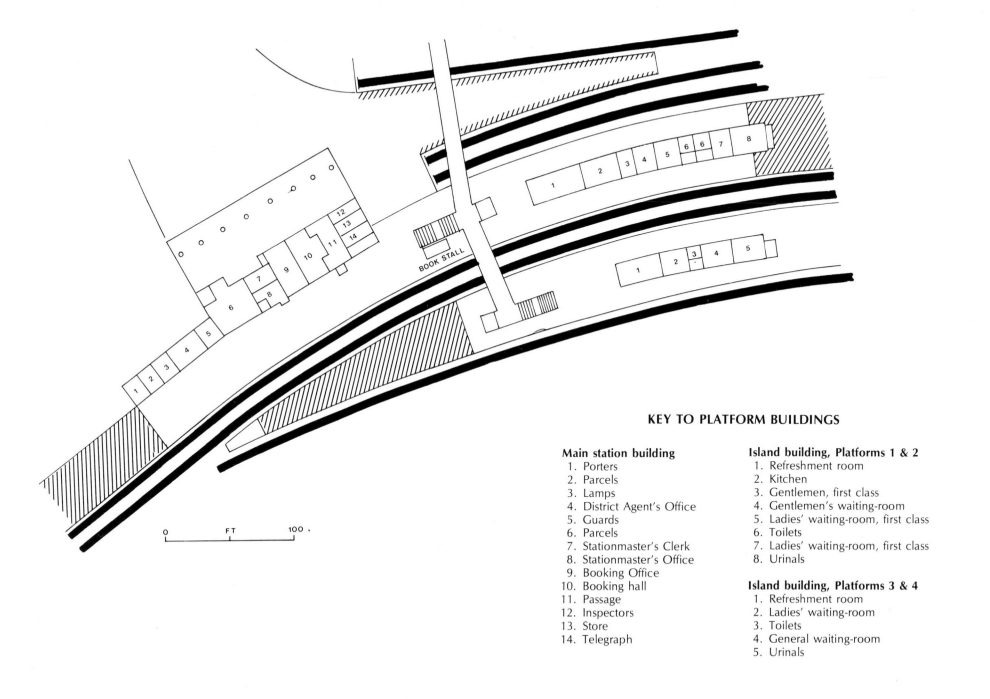

BOOK STALL

0   FT   100

KEY TO PLATFORM BUILDINGS

Main station building
1. Porters
2. Parcels
3. Lamps
4. District Agent's Office
5. Guards
6. Parcels
7. Stationmaster's Clerk
8. Stationmaster's Office
9. Booking Office
10. Booking hall
11. Passage
12. Inspectors
13. Store
14. Telegraph

Island building, Platforms 1 & 2
1. Refreshment room
2. Kitchen
3. Gentlemen, first class
4. Gentlemen's waiting-room
5. Ladies' waiting-room, first class
6. Toilets
7. Ladies' waiting-room, first class
8. Urinals

Island building, Platforms 3 & 4
1. Refreshment room
2. Ladies' waiting-room
3. Toilets
4. General waiting-room
5. Urinals

Gloucester
The buildings on platform 2.

K. White

Gloucester
The new Gloucester Station, in 1983.

Author

Gloucester
Platform 2, after one track had been lifted in 1968.

K. White

Gloucester
Gloucester (Eastgate) Station during demolition in 1977. It reveals the decoration on the wall of the former passage through the building.

H. C. Casserley

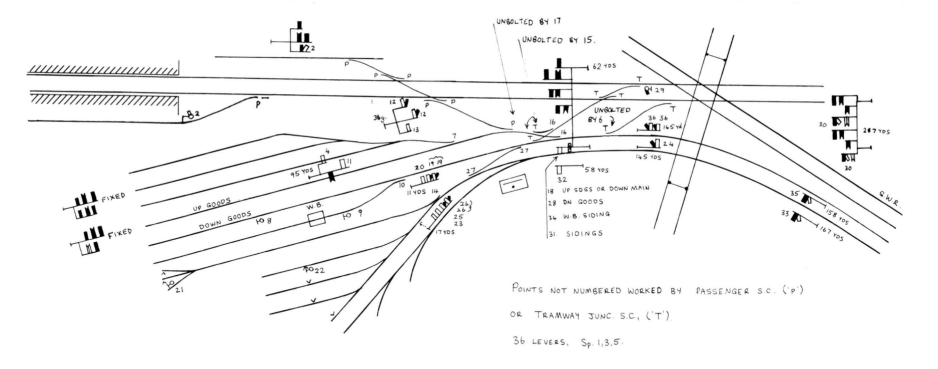

GOODS JUNCTION

POINTS NOT NUMBERED WORKED BY PASSENGER S.C. ('P')

OR TRAMWAY JUNC. S.C. ('T').

36 LEVERS, Sp. 1,3,5.

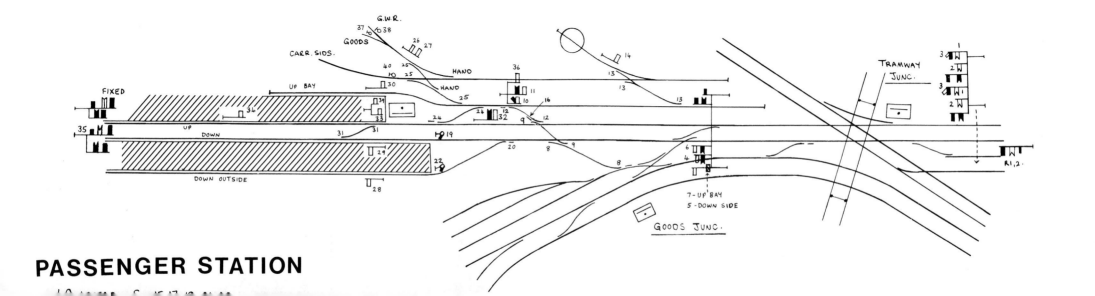

PASSENGER STATION

Gloucester
Pictures of the goods yard in use seem to be non-existent. This is the shed after the tracks had been lifted.

K. White

Gloucester
Gloucester Goods Junction signal box; the last box erected by the LMS to a MR design, in 1924.

HMRS

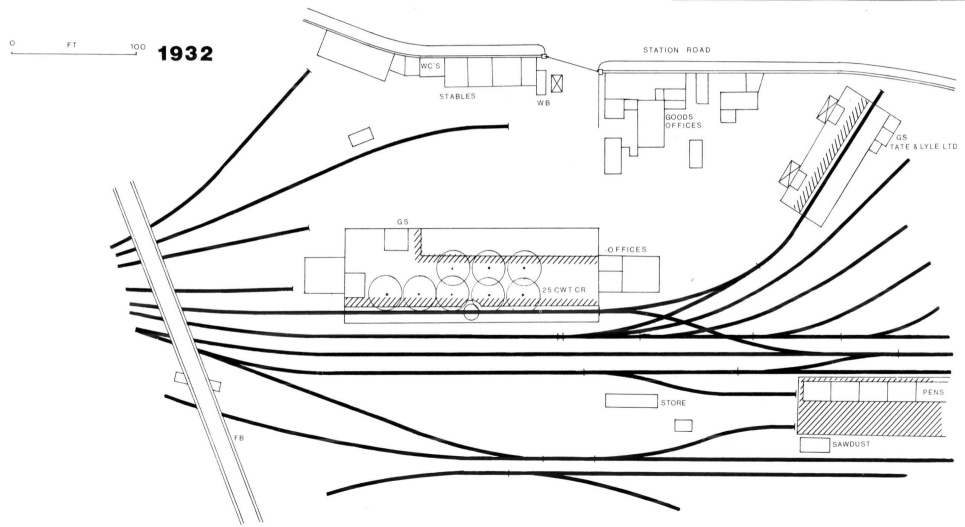

O   FT   100

1932

STATION ROAD

WC'S

STABLES

WB

GOODS OFFICES

GS

.OFFICES

25 CWT CR

GS
TATE & LYLE LTD

STORE

FB

PENS

SAWDUST

PLAN 8: The Barnwood Curve and Engine Shed Junction, after the 1942 quad-rupling. The new locomotive shed was opened in 1895 to replace the old round-house. Known as Gloucester (Barnwood), it was a standard MR brick shed, with a Cowans Sheldon 50ft. turntable. There was a repair shop, a set of shear legs, and a water tower, with an elevated coal stage. The turntable was replaced by a 55ft. table in 1935. Gloucester remained an outstation for repairs until 1923, when it was downgraded; a 1929 proposal to reinstate it was not carried out. The shed became BR (WR) code 85F, and then 85C in 1961 before closure on 4th May 1964.

The sidings at Barnwood were extended between the two plan dates, and Barnwood signal box, shown on the 1880 plan, closed on 10th October 1940, being replaced by a ground frame, as shown. Engine Shed Junction was reinstated in 1901 when the GWR reopened the Cheltenham Loop line. A new signal box was opened in 1942, replacing a MR box of 1894, when the track was quadrupled.

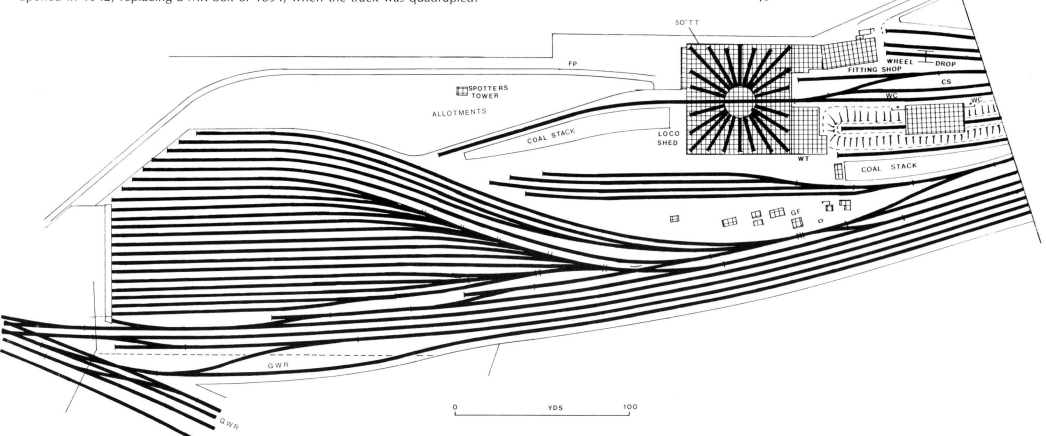

PLAN 8

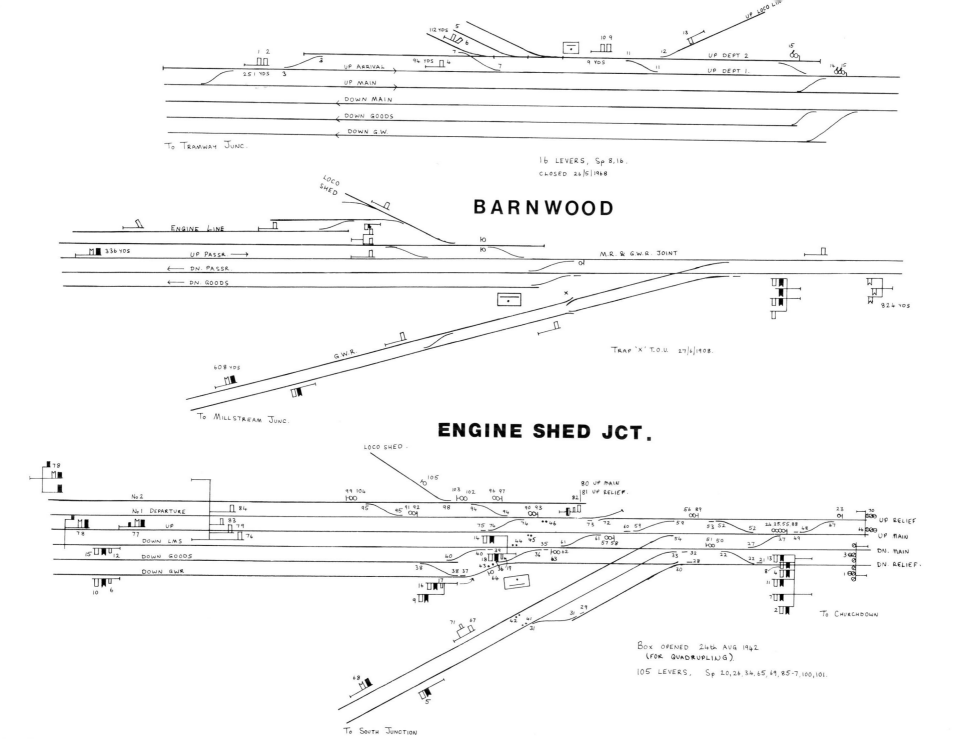

BARNWOOD

To Tramway Junc.

1 2
251 YDS 3
3
UP ARRIVAL
94 YDS 4
UP MAIN
DOWN MAIN
DOWN GOODS
DOWN G.W.

112 YDS 5
6
7
7

9 YDS
10 9
11

UP LOCO LINE
13

12
UP DEPT 2
UP DEPT 1
15
14 15

16 LEVERS, Sp 8,16.
CLOSED 26/5/1968

LOCO SHED

ENGINE LINE
336 YDS
UP PASSR
DN. PASSR.
DN. GOODS

10
10
01

M.R. & G.W.R. JOINT

824 YDS

To Millstream Junc.

608 YDS

G.W.R.

Trap 'X' T.O.U. 27/6/1908.

ENGINE SHED JCT.

To South Junction

LOCO SHED.

No 2
No 1 DEPARTURE
UP
DOWN LMS
DOWN GOODS
DOWN GWR

78
78
77
15 12
10 6

84
95
83 79
76

99 104
100

105
10

103 102 96 97
100 00

98
94

80 UP MAIN
81 UP RELIEF.
82

91 92
95 00
74

90 93
94

44 45 35
14
40 39
40
43 18
38 37
16 17
64
9

46
73 72
61 60 62
36
43
36 19

56 89
00
60 59
59
54
33 32
30
28

53 52
51 50
22
29
31

52
27
23
01

24 25,55,88
0000
27 49
22 21 13

48
3

70
47
66 UP RELIEF
UP MAIN
DN. MAIN
DN. RELIEF.

8 4
11
7 1

2

To Churchdown

71 67
42 41
31

68

5

Box OPENED 24th AUG 1942
(FOR QUADRUPLING).

105 LEVERS, Sp 20,26,34,65,69,85-7,100,101.

39

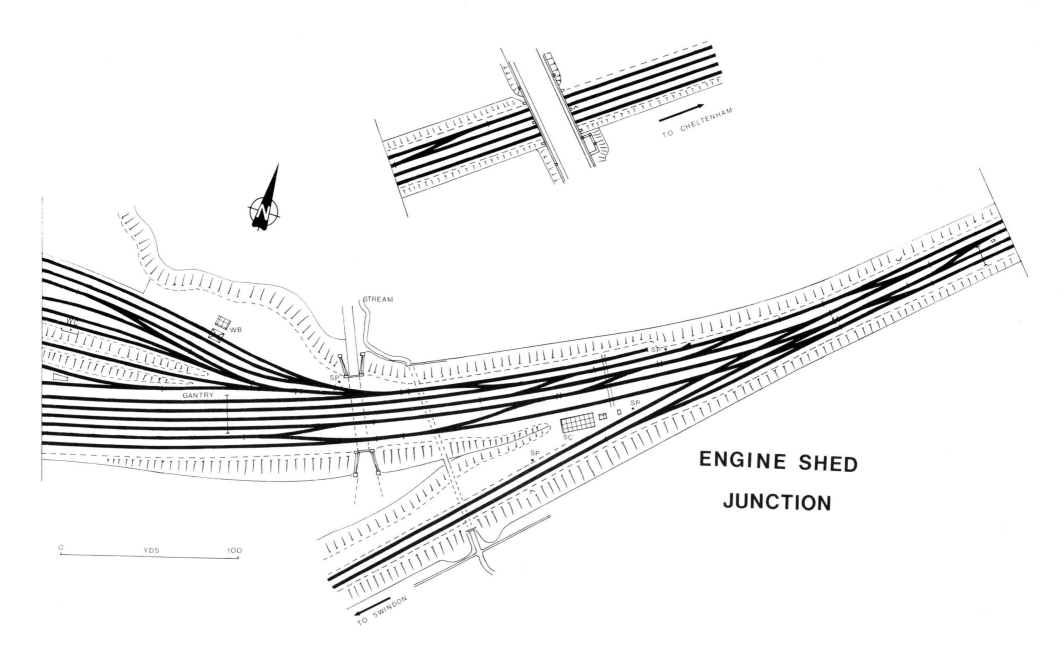

TO CHELTENHAM

STREAM

WC

WB

SP

GANTRY

SP

SP

SC

SP

ENGINE SHED

JUNCTION

YDS   100

TO SWINDON

Gloucester
LMS 0-6-0 locomotive No. 3079, inside the roundhouse.

L&GRP

Gloucester
An LMS 1P 0-4-4T locomotive, No. 1251, outside the shed.

L&GRP

Gloucester
The rear of the engine sheds.

L&GRP

Gloucester
Ex-LMS Beyer-Garratt No. 47927 at Barnwood Shed on 22nd October 1955, with the repair shops beyond.

F. Shuttleworth

Gloucester Docks preceded the opening of the Gloucester & Berkeley Canal; the Port of Gloucester was created by a Charter granted by Queen Elizabeth I, and the docks themselves were opened in 1810. The canal followed in 1827, by which time the port was served by the Cheltenham & Gloucester Railway, which terminated at the Barge Dock of 1812, and served riverside wharves.

When the Birmingham & Gloucester Railway was proposed in 1836, one of the main incentives was the thought of reaching Gloucester Docks and capturing the lucrative Bristol to Birmingham traffic. Through a series of complex negotiations with the C&GWUR, the B&GR bought the tramway, and was thus content for the time being to leave the dock traffic in its hands. When the B&GR reached Gloucester, the station was near the cattle market, and not until 1848 was a connection made to the docks. By this time, the MR had taken over the B&GR, and the GWR was unable to gain access to the docks, despite several tries; at one stage a triple gauge, 3ft. 6in., 4ft. 8½in. and 7ft. 0¼in., line was even suggested.

The GWR eventually reached the docks from the west by way of the Gloucester & Dean Forest Railway, the line being authorised in 1847 and opened about 1852. It was broad gauge until 1869, with a yard to the west of the main basin and connections to the MR line. The gauge was mixed in the docks area until 1872. Agreement was reached between the two companies over working the dock lines in 1875, giving the GWR running powers over the MR lines.

Also in 1875, the Gloucester Railway Wagon & Carriage Company's works was established, and connected to the MR at High Orchard Yard, soon becoming very large, and an important source of traffic.

Many of the internal dock lines were owned by the dock company, and licenced to be worked by the MR and GWR jointly. After 1875, this licence was revoked, and the railways then had to pay the dock company rent for the use of the lines. From 1880, it was agreed that the GWR would work the west side of the docks, and the MR the east. In 1893, the MR obtained powers to build a new line to the west side of the canal, and despite GWR opposition, the line opened in 1898, running from Tuffley Junction to Hempsted Sidings before crossing the canal, and turning north to pass Monks Meadow Dock and join the GWR at Llanthony Yard. This was the last addition to the dock railways, and the first to close, beyond Hempsted, in 1938. The other MR lines all closed in 1971, leaving just the GWR line to serve the docks. Even this is little used.

There is surprisingly little to be seen of the dock railways today; High Orchard Yard has been developed, and only the odd rail can be seen peeping through the worn road surface. The buildings do remain, however, and are well worth a visit in their own right. For a more detailed history of the docks, see the *Bibliography*.

Gloucester
Gloucester Docks.

Author

Gloucester
Gloucester Docks.

Author

Gloucester
Ex-LMS 0-4-0T No. 41537 shunts Gloucester Docks.

G. Robinson

Gloucester
The site of the level crossing of the High Orchard branch over Bristol Road, with the wagon works beyond.

Author

Gloucester
LMS dock tank No. 1540 at High Orchard Sidings.

L&GRP

Gloucester
A special train at the docks on 21st November 1970, in the remains of High Orchard Yard.

H. Ballantyne

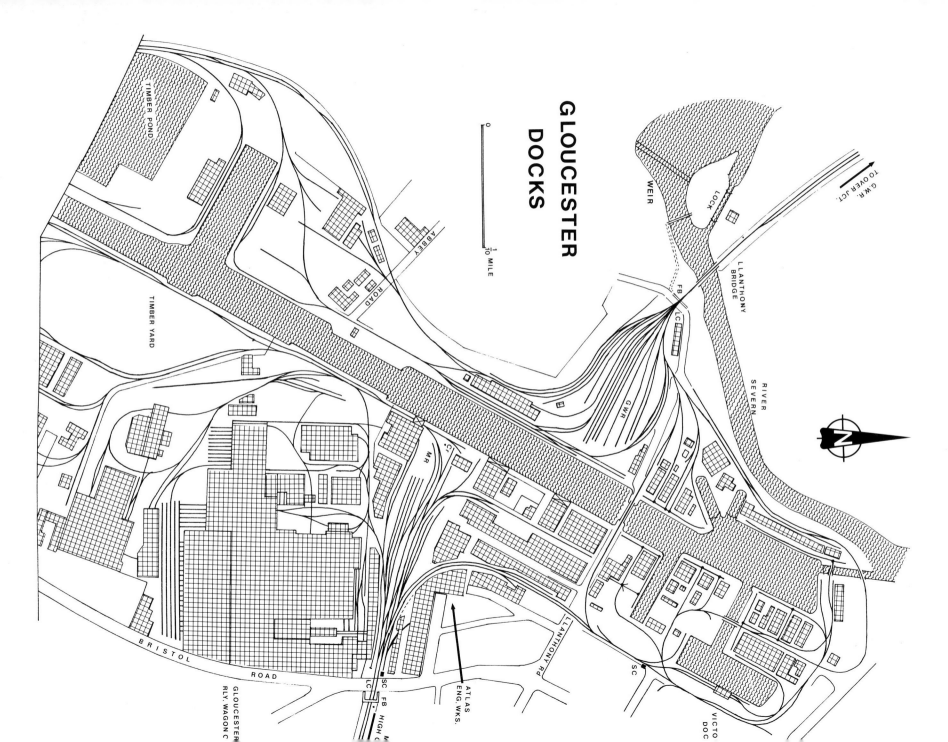

GLOUCESTER DOCKS

0

1/10 MILE

N

TIMBER POND

TIMBER YARD

ABBEY ROAD

WEIR

LOCK

LLANTHONY BRIDGE

RIVER SEVERN

G.W.R. TO OVER JCT.

FB

LC

G W R

MR

CT

BRISTOL ROAD

LLANTHONY RD

ATLAS ENG. WKS.

SC FB HIGH

LC

GLOUCESTER RLY. WAGON C

SC

VICTO DOC

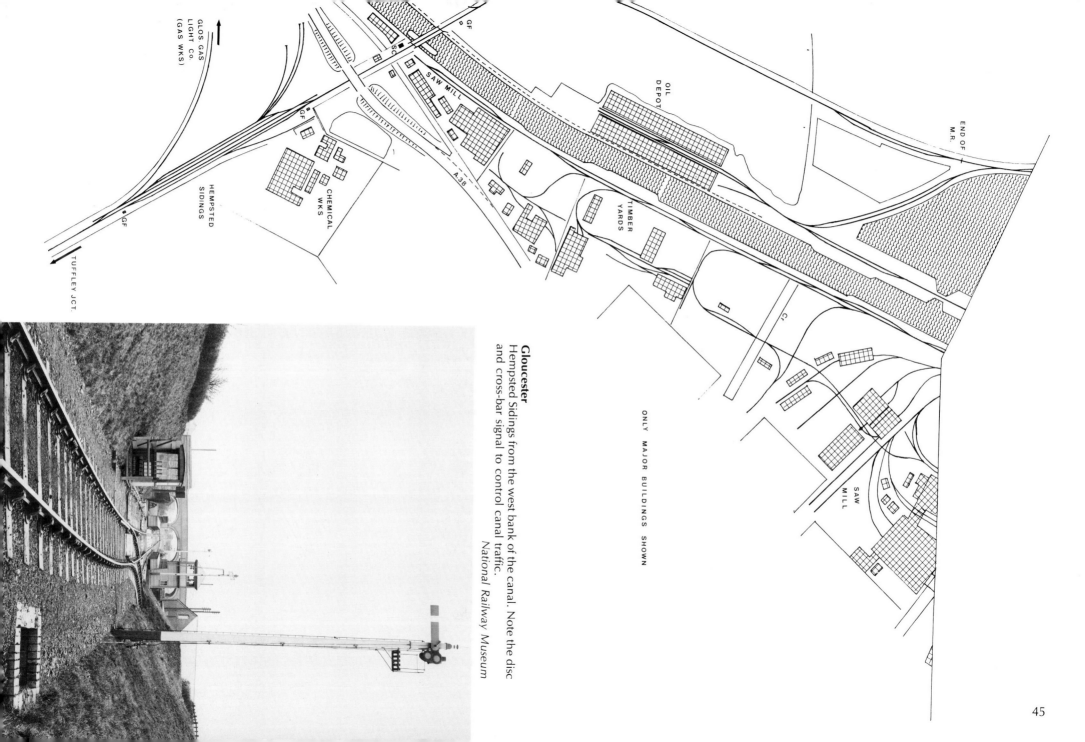

GLOS GAS
LIGHT Co.
(GAS WKS)

GF

HEMPSTED
SIDINGS

TUFFLEY JCT.

GF

CHEMICAL
WKS

GF

SAW MILL

A 38

GF

OIL
DEPOT

END OF
M.R.

TIMBER
YARDS

C

ONLY MAJOR BUILDINGS SHOWN

SAW
MILL

Gloucester
Hempsted Sidings from the west bank of the canal. Note the disc
and cross-bar signal to control Canal traffic.
National Railway Museum

45

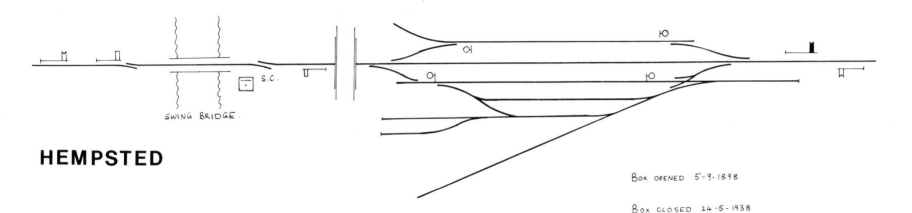

SWING BRIDGE.

S.C.

HEMPSTED

Box opened 5-9-1898

Box closed 24-5-1938

Gloucester

Hempsted signal box, with the canal swing bridge beyond, circa 1920.

National Railway Museum

Gloucester

Hempsted Sidings, on the 1898 New Dock branch, looking towards the canal, with the chemical works on the right, circa 1920.

National Railway Museum

Gloucester
A view looking across the canal from the signal box.

National Railway Museum

Gloucester
Date: 1893; Livery: Black, with white lettering. No. 7 was identical except for yellow lettering.
OPC Collection

Gloucester
Date: circa 1935; Livery: Probably black, lettered white and shaded red.
HMRS

Gloucester
Date: 1886; Livery: Brown, lettered white.
OPC Collection

Gloucester
Date: 1904; Livery: Lead grey, lettered white and shaded black.
OPC Collection

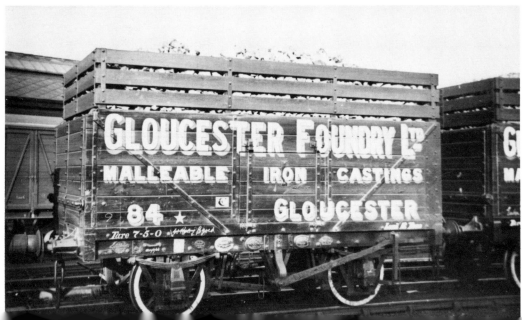

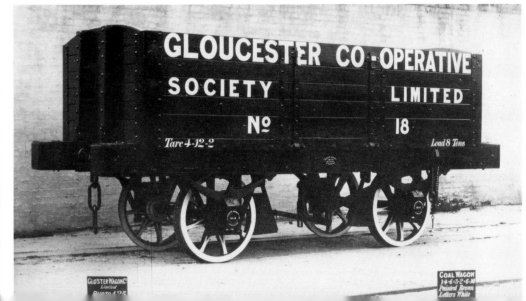

THE BRISTOL & GLOUCESTER RAILWAY

The early history of the B&GR has been covered very fully elsewhere, so I will give only a brief outline here *(see Bibliography)*.

The line had its origins in the Bristol & Gloucestershire Railway, a horse-worked tramway running from coal pits near Westerleigh to the River Avon at Bristol. This line was opened in 1835 throughout, preceding the GWR in Bristol, and was a success in a limited way, but an extension to Gloucester was desirable.

The new line, the Bristol & Gloucester Railway, used the tramway course as far as Westerleigh, and then struck out northwards, skirting the edge of the Cotswold Hills. Engineered by I. K. Brunel, it was built to full broad gauge standards except for the bridges and tunnels, which were somewhat narrow; in most respects, it was indistinguishable from the GWR. At Standish Junction, it joined the Cheltenham & Great Western Union Railway from Swindon, and the B&GR shared their tracks to Gloucester, the lines also sharing the Gloucester Station, as covered in the last section.

The Bristol & Gloucester Railway was a typical Brunel creation, with stations like those on the GWR with cottage like buildings in a Gothic style, with wide awnings and tall chimneys. Track layouts were simple *(see Appendix 1)*, and the line opened to passenger traffic on 8th July 1844, following an official opening on Saturday, 6th. Goods traffic commenced on 2nd September.

It was obvious at once that the main traffic flow was north to south, and the break of gauge at Gloucester was the cause of much delay. Despite this, the two B&GRs combined in 1845 to form the Bristol & Birmingham Railway. At this stage, everyone expected the line to become a part of the rapidly expanding GWR empire, but through a mixture of luck and good judgement, the MR secured it instead, giving them an entry into the heart of GWR territory at Bristol. Thus, a typical GWR broad gauge line was to become familiar with the products of Derby Works, the Brunel stations being complemented by the addition of MR signal boxes, etc.

The MR lost little time in developing their new acquisition. As early as 1846, suggestions were being made towards improving the stations, and in 1847 houses were built at Yate, Wickwar, Charfield, Frocester and Stonehouse. A house had been built at Berkeley Road in 1844, to a different design. At the same time, the yard side of all the goods sheds except Frocester was enclosed by wooden panels with sliding doors, protecting the goods and those loading them. The sheds had a small crane and a weighing machine inside, only Charfield ever needing a larger yard crane. The details of the stations in 1844 are covered in *Appendix 1*.

The idea of sharing the line to Gloucester with the GWR north of Standish did not appeal to the MR, and on 22nd May 1854, a new line was opened parallel with the GWR, from Standish to Gloucester. This was of standard gauge, and the remainder of the line was standardised at the same time, although the third rail remained, unused, until 1872, due to an agreement with the GWR. The MR also had to go on paying the GWR rent for the use of the Standish to Gloucester section until the 20 year agreement, signed in 1844, ran out.

Later developments on the line are dealt with in the text accompanying the plans.

TIMETABLE FOR BRISTOL TO GLOUCESTER LINE (From 1st March 1847)

BRISTOL	05.45	08.15	11.00	01.40	05.00	06.55	06.43	05.00	06.55
MANGOTSFIELD	–	08.30	11.12	–	05.16	–	07.00	05.15	–
YATE	06.06	08.41	11.25	02.03	05.28	07.20	07.12	05.27	07.20
WICKWAR	–	08.55	–	–	05.40	–	07.24	05.39	–
CHARFIELD	06.25	09.01	11.41	02.22	05.50	07.39	07.30	05.45	07.30
BERKELEY ROAD	06.38	09.15	11.54	02.34	06.02	07.52	07.42	05.57	07.52
FROCESTER	–	09.28	12.06	–	06.14	–	07.52	06.07	–
STONEHOUSE	06.53	09.34	12.10	02.48	06.26	08.05	07.58	06.13	08.05
GLOUCESTER	07.20	10.15	12.45	03.25	07.15	08.50	08.40	06.35	08.50
	a.m.	a.m.	a.m.	p.m.	p.m.	p.m.	a.m.	p.m.	p.m.
M = Mail	1&2	1&2	1&2M	1&2	1,2&3	1&2M	1,2&3	1,2&3	1&2M

SUNDAYS

GLOUCESTER	04.20	07.50	10.40	02.05	04.40	09.05	04.20	10.00	08.15
STONEHOUSE	04.42	08.10	11.00	02.25	05.00	09.25	04.42	10.20	08.35
FROCESTER	–	08.15	11.05	–	05.05	–	–	10.25	08.40
BERKELEY ROAD	04.57	08.28	11.17	02.40	05.20	09.40	04.57	10.38	08.53
CHARFIELD	05.11	08.40	11.29	02.52	05.27	09.50	05.11	10.50	09.05
WICKWAR		08.45	11.34	02.57				10.55	09.10
YATE	–	08.56	11.47	03.08	05.43	10.06	–	11.06	09.21
MANGOTSFIELD	–	09.10	12.00	03.20	05.55	–	–	11.20	09.35
BRISTOL	05.50	09.30	12.20	03.40	06.15	10.30	05.50	11.45	10.00
	a.m.	a.m.	a.m.	p.m.	p.m.	p.m.	a.m.	p.m.	p.m.
	1&2M	1&2M	1,2&3	1&2M	1&2	1&2	1&2	1,2&3	1,2&3

SUNDAYS

Day return tickets available at every station, (cannot be used on 08.15 ex-Bristol if 2nd class)

50

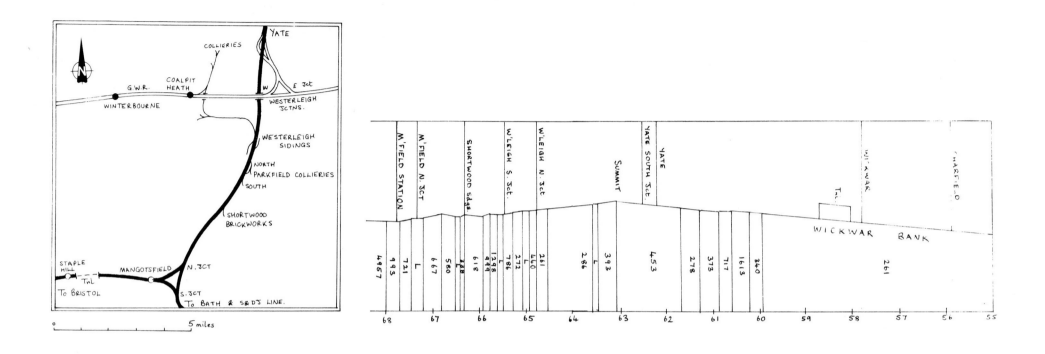

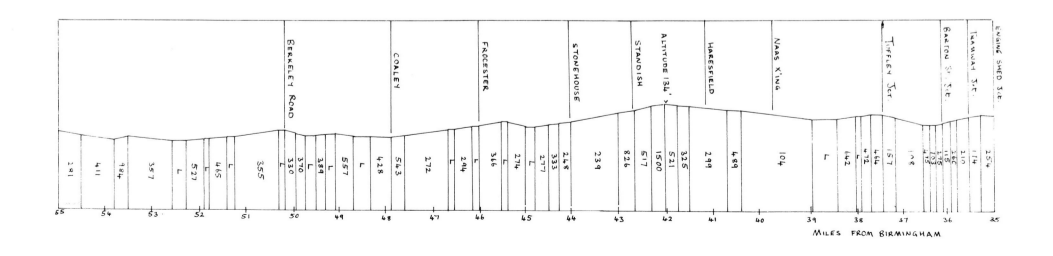

MILES FROM BIRMINGHAM

Opened: Original station, circa 1846
          New station, 4th August 1869
Closed: 7th March 1966

The junction at Mangotsfield dated from the opening of the Bristol & Gloucestershire and Avon & Gloucester tramways, opened to here in 1831. The two lines met here, and ran north as one line to the Coalpit Heath pits. At that time it was called Keynsham Junction, after the town on the River Avon near where the A&GR terminated. When the B&GR became a railway in 1844, mixed gauge track was laid so the A&GR could retain access to the coalfield, but there was endless trouble with the poorly maintained tramway, and trying to combine locomotive and horse working. Before long, the tramway terminated at Mangotsfield. It closed as a through route in 1865.

No station was built here when the B&GR opened, but it was resolved in 1845 to build a station to serve the area on the cheapest scale, this opening soon afterwards. A brick station building stood separately from the platforms, which were uncovered; the 'up' platform received a shelter in 1848. The station remained thus until 1869.

In that year, the important line to Bath was opened. First suggested in 1846, it was more of a main line than a branch, especially after the S&DJR opened its Bath extension. A triangle was built at Mangotsfield, and a new junction station was built nearer Bristol, the old station being on the site of the new North Junction. The station was an important interchange point, generating little local traffic; there were four main platforms, with a bay on the Bath line. The buildings were poor, only providing the minimum of facilities, although the platforms were covered with wide awnings. These preceded the evolution of the familiar MR design, and were rather austere. The platforms were joined by a subway.

The station was opened for goods on 1st September 1869, although little goods traffic was ever handled.

The station became extremely busy, especially after the Bath line was upgraded in the 1930s to allow the use of heavier locomotives but, in the 1950s, traffic began to decline, leading to closure.

Mangotsfield South Junction had lost its signal box as early as 6th October 1935. On 18th September 1962, the north to south loop was closed to passenger trains, following the rerouting of the principal named train, the 'Pines Express'. The carriage sidings at North Junction were closed from 12th September 1965, and then on 7th March 1966, the Bath line was closed to passengers, and Mangotsfield Station closed. The signal box was burnt down on 29th January 1967, and was not replaced; all the points were removed, leaving just plain main line. The line closed on 29th December 1969, only a single line remaining north of North Junction as far as Yate . . . this connected to the Bath line until complete closure on 28th May 1971. The line remains today for the training of track machine drivers.

The station has been stripped of its canopies, but the stone buildings and platforms remain. Mangotsfield was a bleak, unwelcoming station; the writer Arnold Ridley is said to have received inspiration for his story *The Ghost Train* while waiting for a connection there one winter's night.

Mangotsfield
The original Mangotsfield Station together with North Junction signal box.

C. Maggs

Mangotsfield
LMS 4-6-0 'Jubilee' No. 5606 *Falkland Islands* with indicator shelters, enters Mangotsfield from the north, circa 1938.

L&GRP

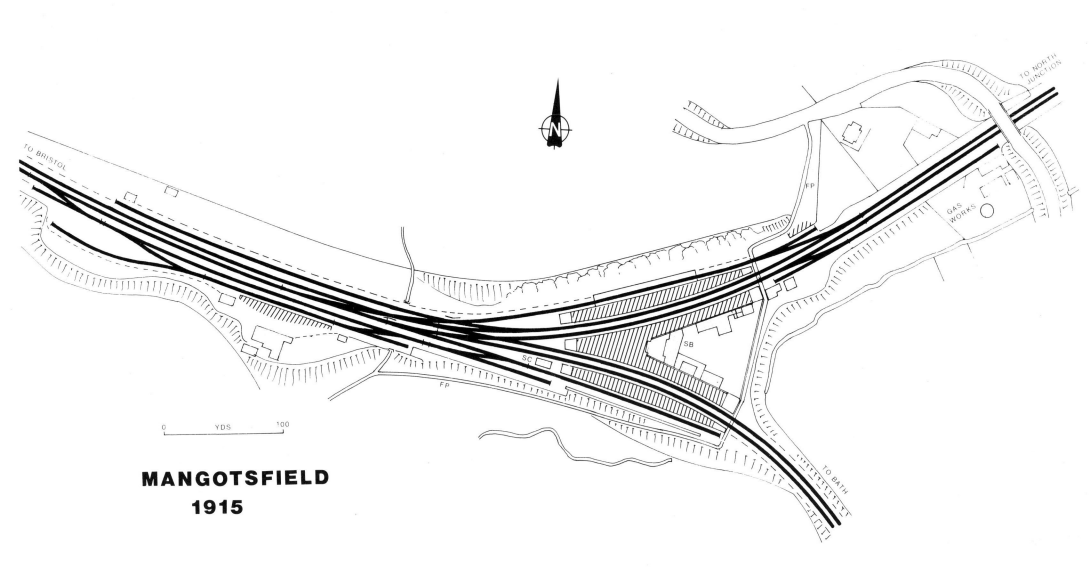

TO BRISTOL

TO NORTH JUNCTION

FP

GAS WORKS

SB

SC

FP

TO BATH

0 YDS 100

MANGOTSFIELD
1915

Mangotsfield
The Gloucester line platforms, circa 1960.

Lens of Sutton

Mangotsfield
Mangotsfield in 1947.

L&GRP

Mangotsfield
Mangotsfield was a very bleak station, as this view emphasises.

Lens of Sutton

Mangotsfield
The Bath line platforms.

C. Maggs

Mangotsfield
The 'up' 'Cornishman' leaves Mangotsfield behind ex-GWR 'Castle' No. 5061 *Earl of Birkenhead* on 21st April 1961.

Author's Collection

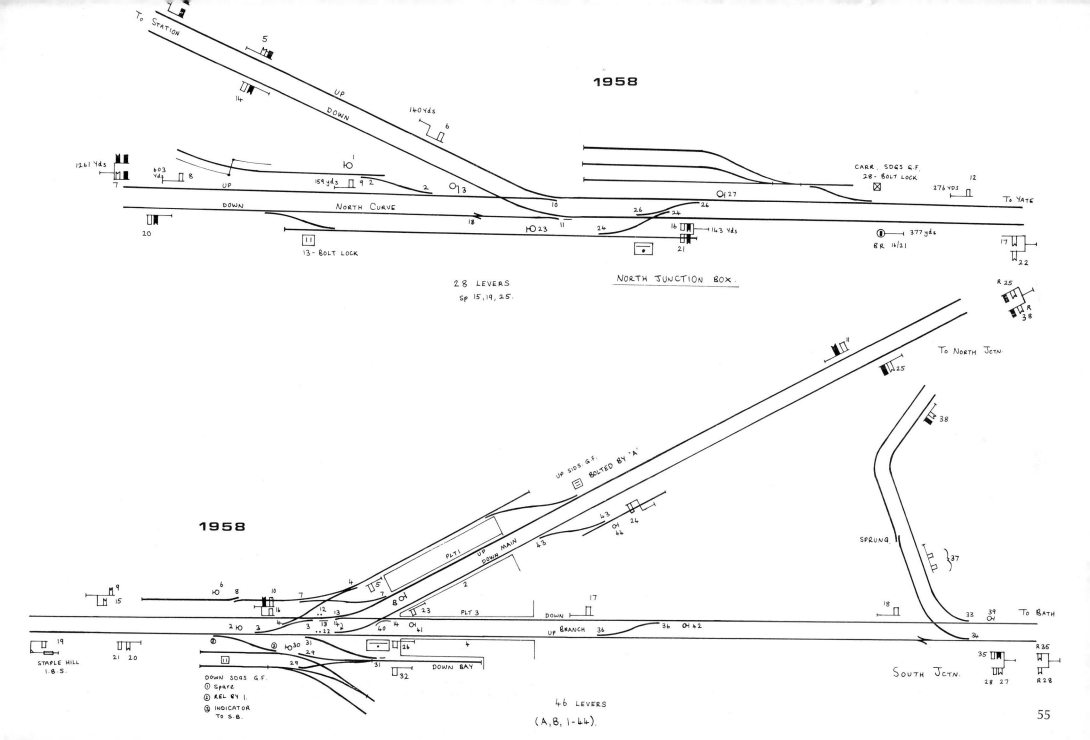

1958

To STATION

5

UP
DOWN

14

140 Yds
6

1261 Yds
7

603 Yds
8

1

159 Yds 9 2

2

3

10

18

UP

DOWN   NORTH CURVE

11

23

24

26 24 26

27

CARR. SDGS G.F.
28 - BOLT LOCK

12

276 YDS

TO YATE

20

13 - BOLT LOCK

24

16

143 Yds

21

377 yds

BR 16/21

17
22

28 LEVERS
SP 15, 19, 25.

NORTH JUNCTION BOX.

R 25

R
38

1958

TO NORTH JCTN.

11

25

38

UP SIDS. G.F.
BOLTED BY 'A'

SPRUNG

37

43
24
44

PLT1
UP
DOWN MAIN   43

2

9
15

6
8

10

16

4
7

5
7

8

12 13

23

PLT 3

17

DOWN

18

33 39

TO BATH

2
3

4

3 13 4
22

40 4

41

UP BRANCH   36

36   42

34

19
STAPLE HILL
I.B.S.

21 20

30 31

29

31

4

11

29

32

26

DOWN BAY

35
28 27

R 35

R 28

SOUTH JCTN.

DOWN SDGS G.F.
① Spare
② REL BY I.
③ INDICATOR
   TO S.B.

46 LEVERS

(A, B, 1-44).

55

BRIDGE AT MANGOTSFIELD

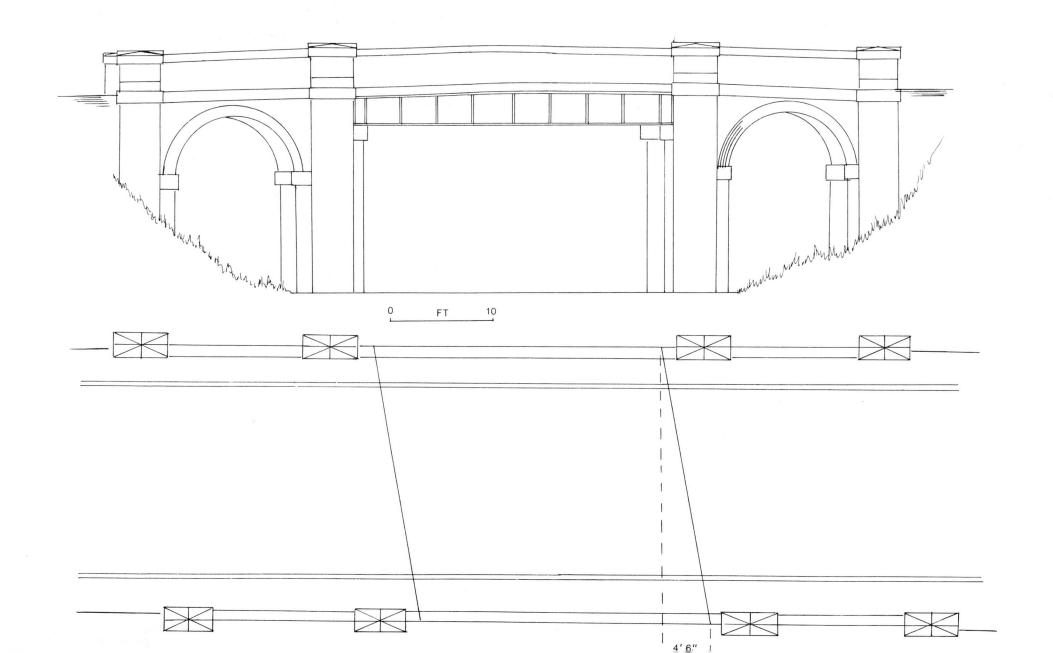

0　FT　10

4' 6"

Mangotsfield
The original B&GR bridge north of Mangotsfield, circa 1890, with North Junction beyond.
It was replaced soon after by the bridge shown in the drawings.

National Railway Museum

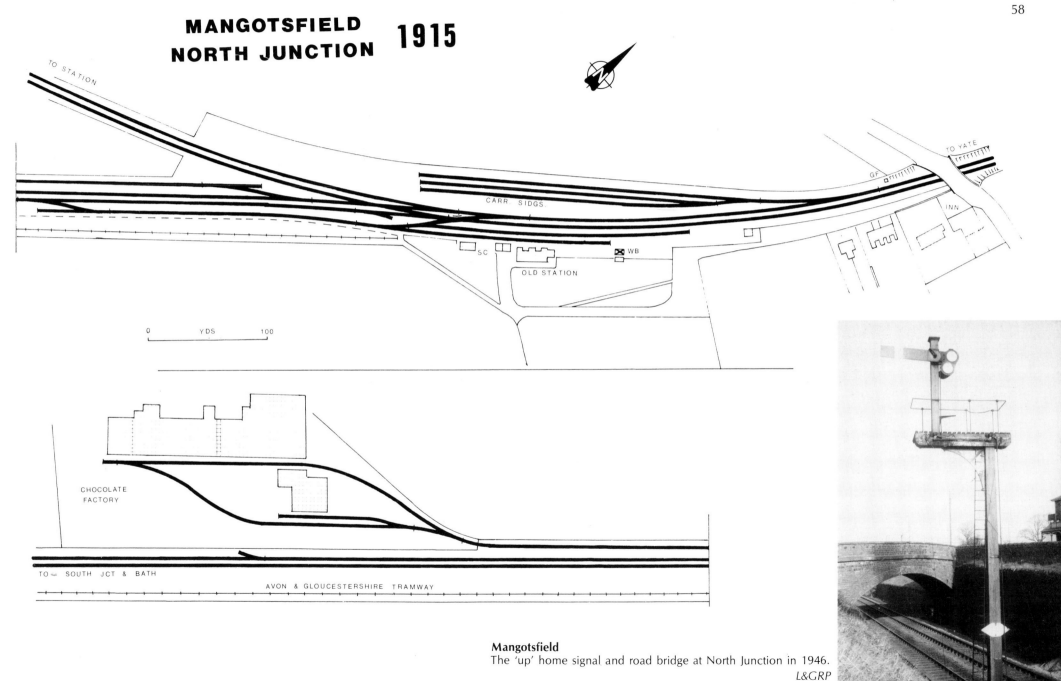

MANGOTSFIELD NORTH JUNCTION **1915**

58

TO STATION

TO YATE

GF

INN

CARR. SIDGS.

SC

OLD STATION

WB

0 YDS 100

CHOCOLATE FACTORY

TO SOUTH JCT & BATH

AVON & GLOUCESTERSHIRE TRAMWAY

Mangotsfield
The 'up' home signal and road bridge at North Junction in 1946.
L&GRP

SHORTWOOD BRICKWORKS

The brickworks at Shortwood was served by sidings controlled from Shortwood signal box. The first connection was in broad gauge days, to Shortwood Colliery, but this closed about 1870, and the brickworks was established next to the main line. There was a signal box there by 1872; a very early installation. The works was owned by the Cattybrook Brick Co., the firm owning a fleet of private owner wagons. The sidings and signal box closed on 22nd February 1965.

SHORTWOOD 1915

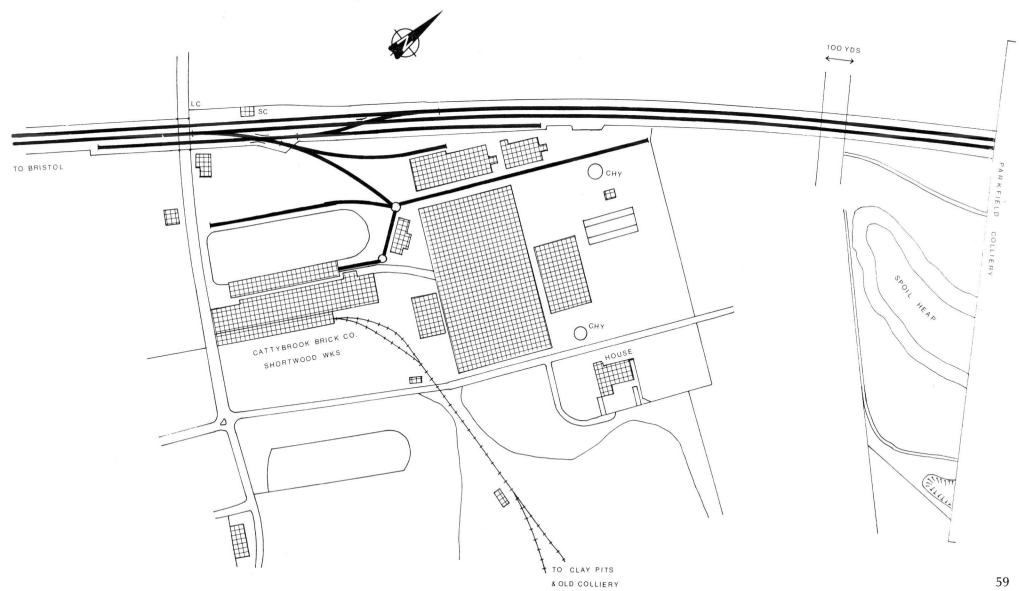

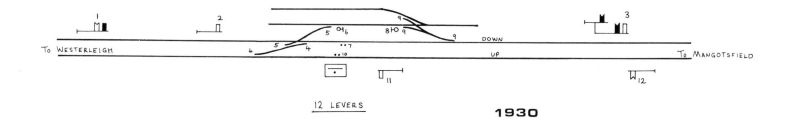

12 LEVERS

1930

SHORTWOOD

1872

LAYOUT NEWLY INTERLOCKED

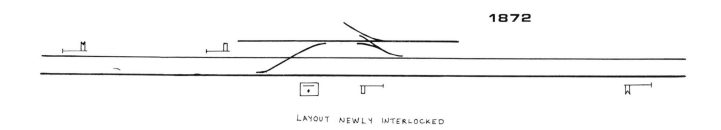

Shortwood
The Cattybrook Brick Co. works at Shortwood, circa 1920, with a train of MR wagons in the siding.

Cattybrook Brick Co.

Shortwood
Three wagons as rebuilt in 1926. The livery seems to be black, with the lettering in white.

OPC Collection

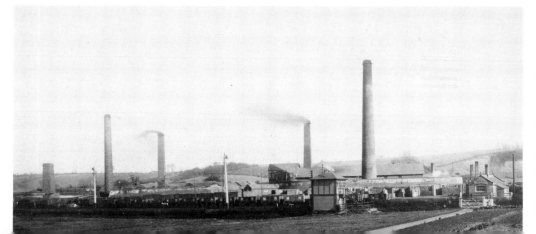

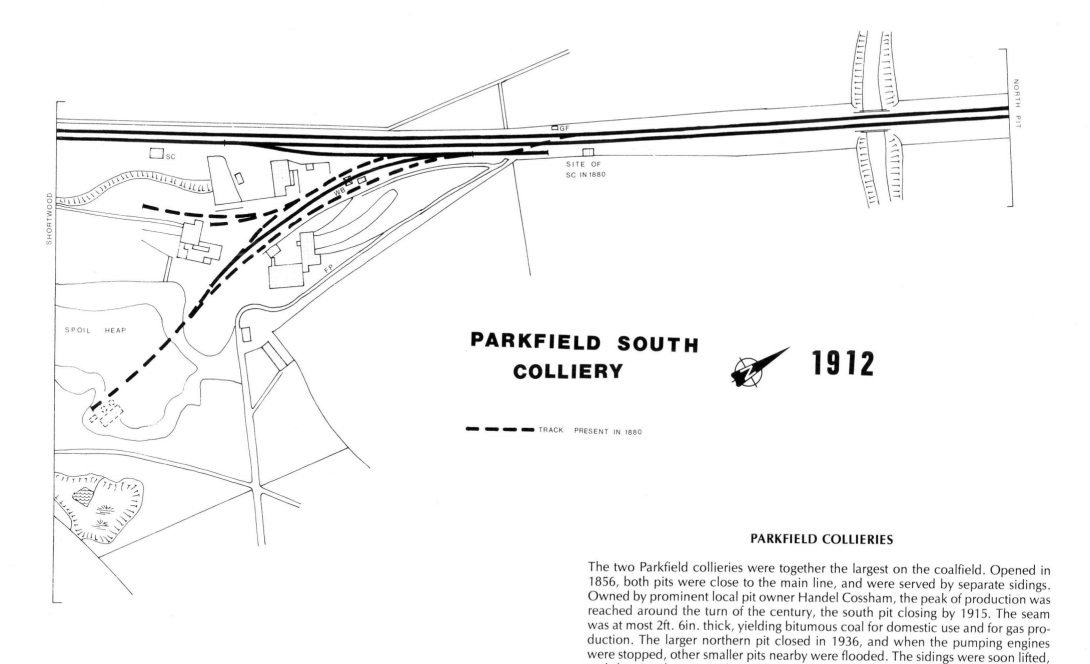

PARKFIELD SOUTH COLLIERY

1912

– – – – – TRACK PRESENT IN 1880

SHORTWOOD

NORTH PIT

SC

SITE OF
SC IN 1880

GF

WB

FP

SPOIL HEAP

PARKFIELD COLLIERIES

The two Parkfield collieries were together the largest on the coalfield. Opened in 1856, both pits were close to the main line, and were served by separate sidings. Owned by prominent local pit owner Handel Cossham, the peak of production was reached around the turn of the century, the south pit closing by 1915. The seam was at most 2ft. 6in. thick, yielding bitumous coal for domestic use and for gas production. The larger northern pit closed in 1936, and when the pumping engines were stopped, other smaller pits nearby were flooded. The sidings were soon lifted, and the sites have now been cleared.

61

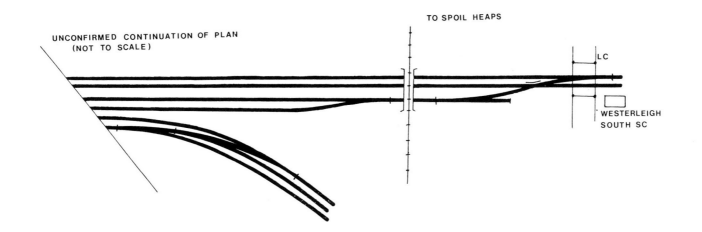

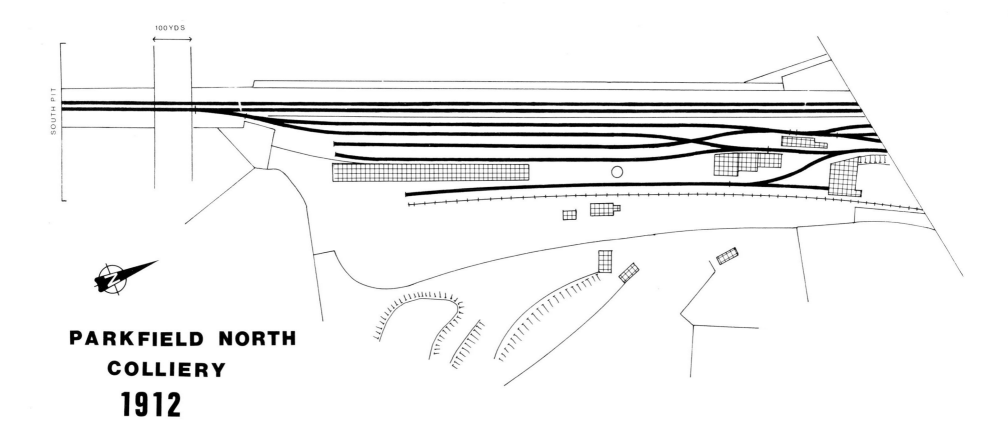

62

100 YDS

SOUTH PIT

PARKFIELD NORTH
COLLIERY
1912

TO SPOIL HEAPS

UNCONFIRMED CONTINUATION OF PLAN
(NOT TO SCALE)

LC

WESTERLEIGH
SOUTH SC

WESTERLEIGH SIDINGS AND THE COALPIT HEATH BRANCH

The original main line of the B&G Tramway terminated at collieries around Coalpit Heath, the line being built to give these pits access to the port of Bristol. When the railway was built, the line to the pits became a branch, and Westerleigh Junction was created. In B&GR days, a branch on the 'down' side of the main line served Dudley pit, which soon closed, but the other collieries on the main branch produced large quantities of coal, despite their small sizes and the thin coal seam. The original line ran to Serridge pit via New Engine Yard, where a line branched off to the north to serve Frog Lane and Mayshill pits, the MR being responsible for maintaining it only as far as New Engine Yard.

A large yard was built at Westerleigh by the MR at the end of the 19th century, which relieved the congested sidings in Bristol, and allowed the sorting of traffic for the Bath line. Controlled from four signal boxes, the yard was south of the branch junction, with separate 'up' and 'down' sidings, which were lengthened in 1940, extra sidings being added in 1942.

Traffic over the mineral line ceased in 1949, although part of the line remained for wagon storage. Westerleigh Sidings closed on 22nd February 1965, and were soon lifted, having been relatively little used for some time. The main line was closed to ordinary traffic, and singled, on 3rd January 1970.

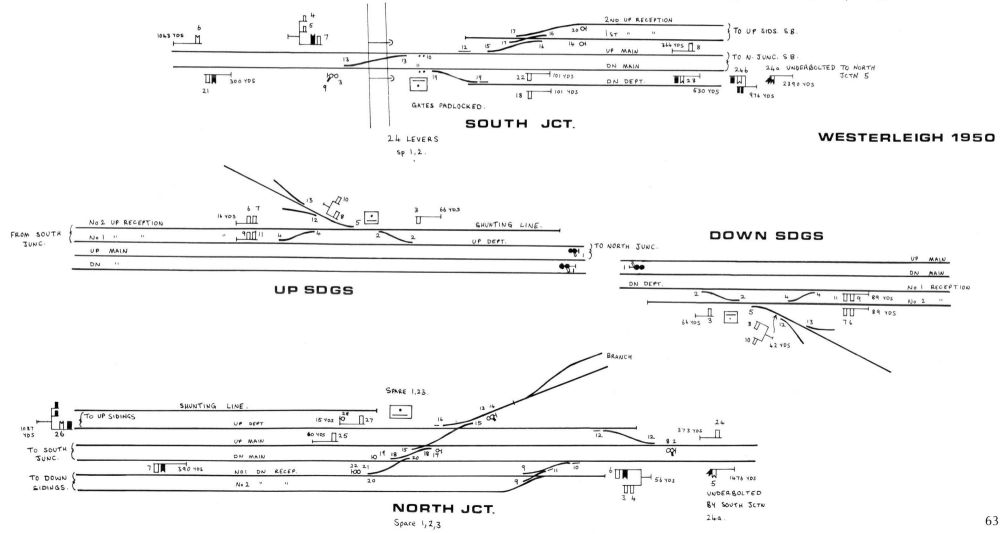

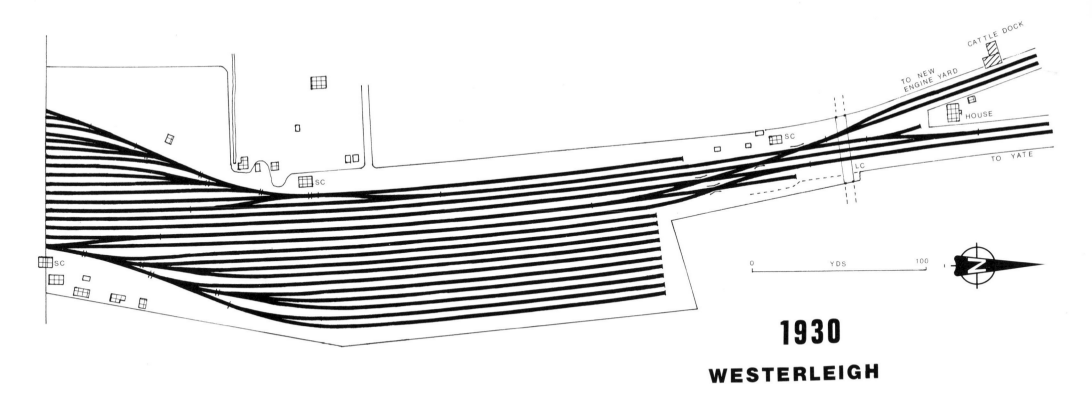

CATTLE DOCK

TO NEW
ENGINE YARD

HOUSE

TO YATE

SC

SC

LC

SC

SC

0   YDS   100

1930

WESTERLEIGH

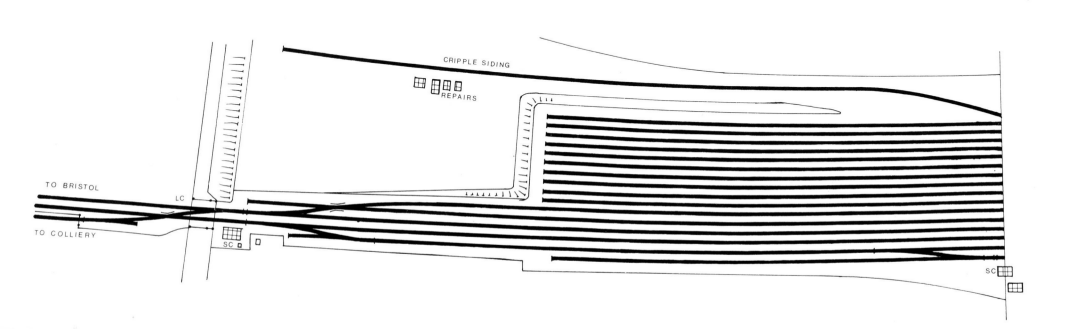

CRIPPLE SIDING

REPAIRS

TO BRISTOL

LC

TO COLLIERY

SC

SC

SC

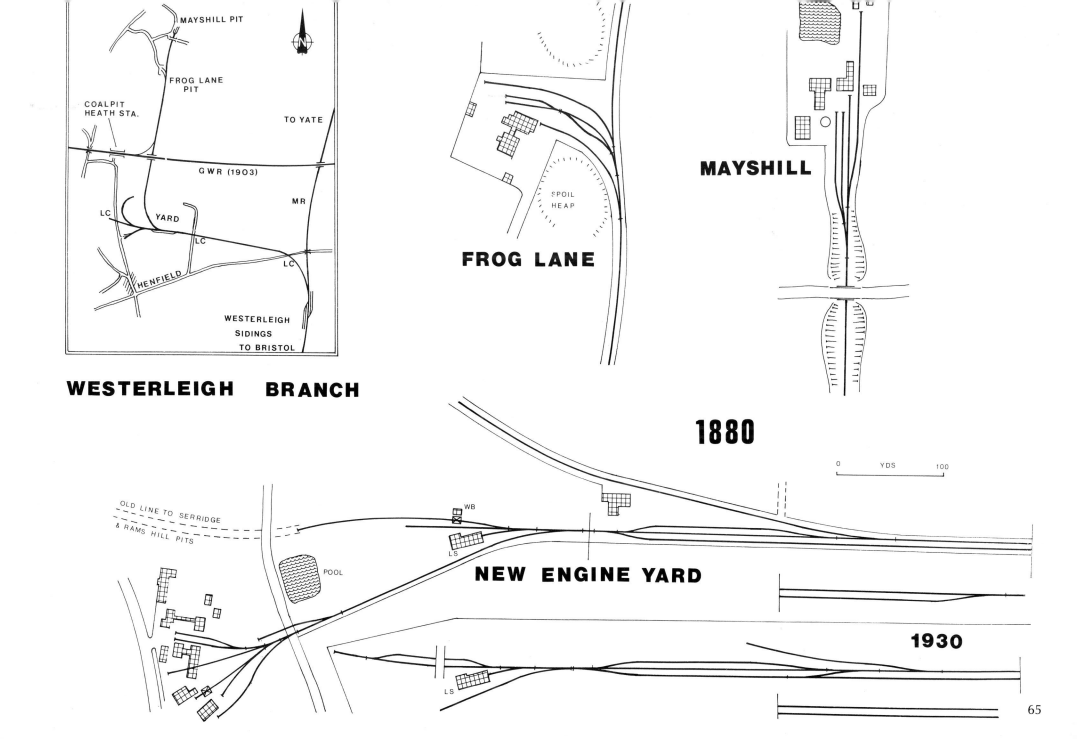

MAYSHILL PIT

FROG LANE PIT

COALPIT HEATH STA.

TO YATE

GWR (1903)

MR

LC

YARD

LC

LC

HENFIELD

WESTERLEIGH SIDINGS

TO BRISTOL

WESTERLEIGH BRANCH

FROG LANE

SPOIL HEAP

MAYSHILL

1880

0   YDS   100

OLD LINE TO SERRIDGE & RAMS HILL PITS

WB

LS

NEW ENGINE YARD

POOL

1930

LS

TO BRISTOL

TO G.W.R.

SC

YATE STATION

YATE SOUTH (NOT TO SCALE)

MR

MR

YATE

YATE SOUTH
JUNCTION

GWR

GWR

EAST

WEST

WESTERLEIGH
JUNCTION

Yate
LMS Compound No. 1002 passes Yate South, with the signal box on the left and the station beyond.

L&GRP

Yate
A 4-6-0 'County' class locomotive crosses the MR line at Yate with a Bristol train.

R. Blencowe

Opened: (Station), 6th July 1844; Public, 8th July 1844;
                                        Goods, 2nd September 1844
                (Branch) 2nd September 1872
Closed: (Station) 4th January 1965
                (Branch) Passengers, 19th June 1944;
                                 Goods, 3rd September, 1967
Reopened: (Branch) 3rd July 1972

Yate was one of the six original stations on the Bristol & Gloucester Railway. At first, it was a small affair, with two short platforms adjacent to a road overbridge. A square goods shed stood near the bridge, served by a siding from a wagon turntable, from which other sidings radiated. Beyond the bridge, a loop served a wharf for loading iron ore, carted from Frampton Quarries.

The buildings were of typical Brunel design, in brick, with stone decoration, and wide canopies over the platforms. The goods shed had an internal loading platform, and a small lean-to office. The yard side of the shed was enclosed, in 1847, at which time a house was built for the clerk.

On 22nd May 1854, the gauge was narrowed, although the layout remained unchanged until 1872, when a branch was opened to Thornbury. The junction was north of the bridge, a turntable being provided, with extra sidings; no bay platforms were built as the branch trains ran through to Bristol. The 'up' platform was lengthened and a footbridge was built around 1890.

The importance of Yate increased again in 1908, when Yate South Junction was opened to provide a connection to the new GWR South Wales direct line, opened in 1903. The junction opened on 9th March 1908, and GWR trains began to use the MR line between Standish and Yate.

The Thornbury line lost its passenger service on 19th June 1944, and Yate Station itself closed on 4th January 1965. The main line south of Yate South was closed on 29th December 1969, all trains using the connection to the GWR line; the junction was realigned on 18th January 1970, and this arrangement remains in use today. The three signal boxes at Yate closed as follows: Station box on 20th October 1969; South Junction box on 10th May 1971, and Single Line Junction box, on the branch, in 1924, this becoming a ground frame. The branch, after closure to goods on 3rd September 1967, was reopened for stone trains from Grovesend Quarry, on 3rd July 1972, using lifted track from the Bath line.

Sadly, of the buildings at Yate, only the goods shed remains at the time of writing, in derelict condition.

Yate
Yate Station, circa 1920, showing the road bridge before it was widened. The footbridge is painted cream and brown. The track is still inside keyed.

National Railway Museum

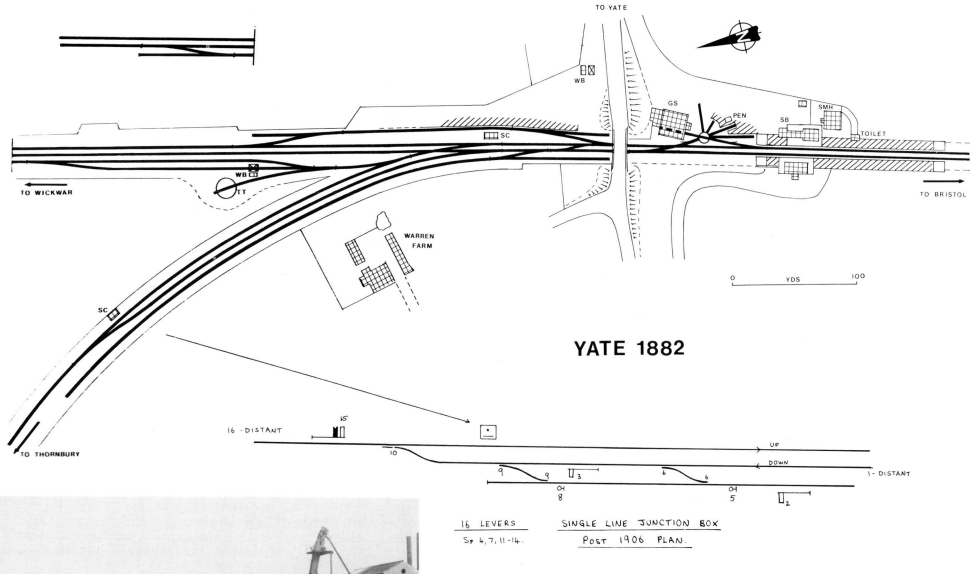

TO YATE

WB

GS

PEN

SB

SMH

TOILET

SC

WB

TT

TO WICKWAR

TO BRISTOL

WARREN
FARM

0   YDS   100

YATE 1882

SC

TO THORNBURY

16 - DISTANT

15

10

UP

DOWN

1 - DISTANT

9   9   3   6   6

8   5   2

16 LEVERS   SINGLE LINE JUNCTION BOX

Sp 4,7, 11 -14.   POST 1906 PLAN.

Yate
The junction of the Thornbury line, with the Parnell Aircraft Works on the right.
C. Maggs

Yate
Yate, in 1932, photographed from the bridge. Note the lengthened 'up' platform.

L&GRP

YATE

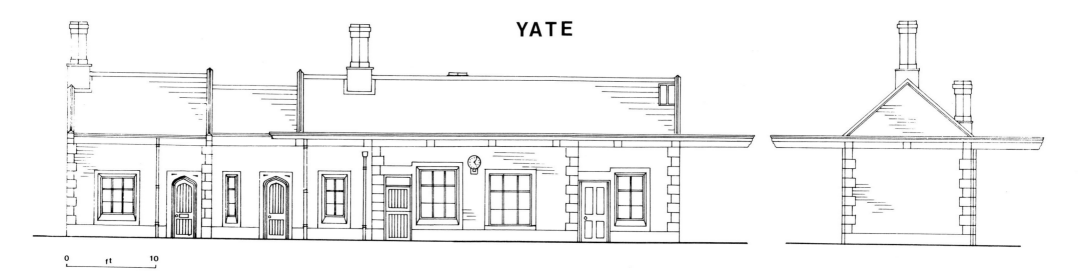

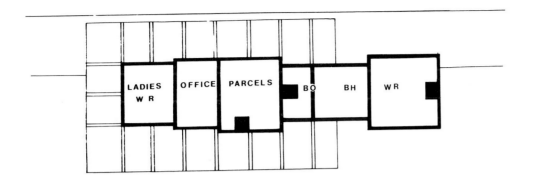

LADIES W R | OFFICE | PARCELS | BO | BH | W R

YATE
JUNCTION FOR
THORNBURY

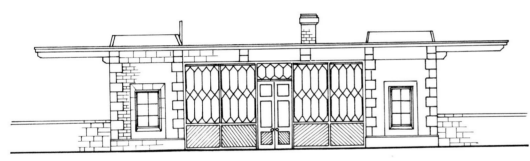

0   1   2   3   4 Ft

0   10 FT

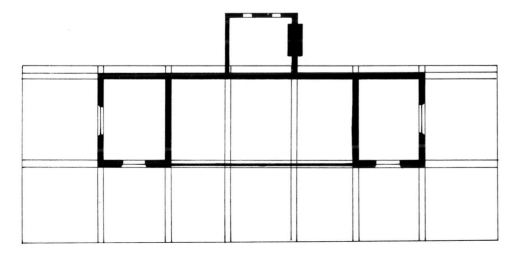

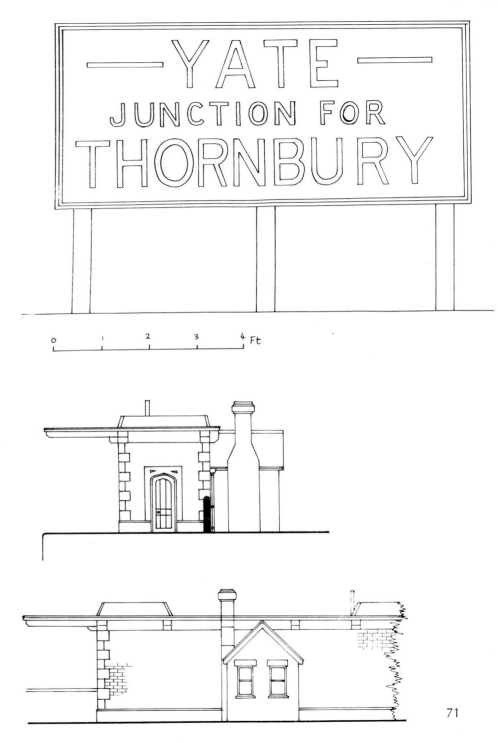

71

Yate
Yate Station at the turn of century.

Author's Collection

Yate
Yate station, circa 1960.

Lens of Sutton

Yate
A view from the 'up' platform, showing the signal box through the bridge.

Lens of Sutton

Yate
'Spinner' No. 77 at Yate, circa 1920, showing the wagon turntable in detail.

Author's Collection

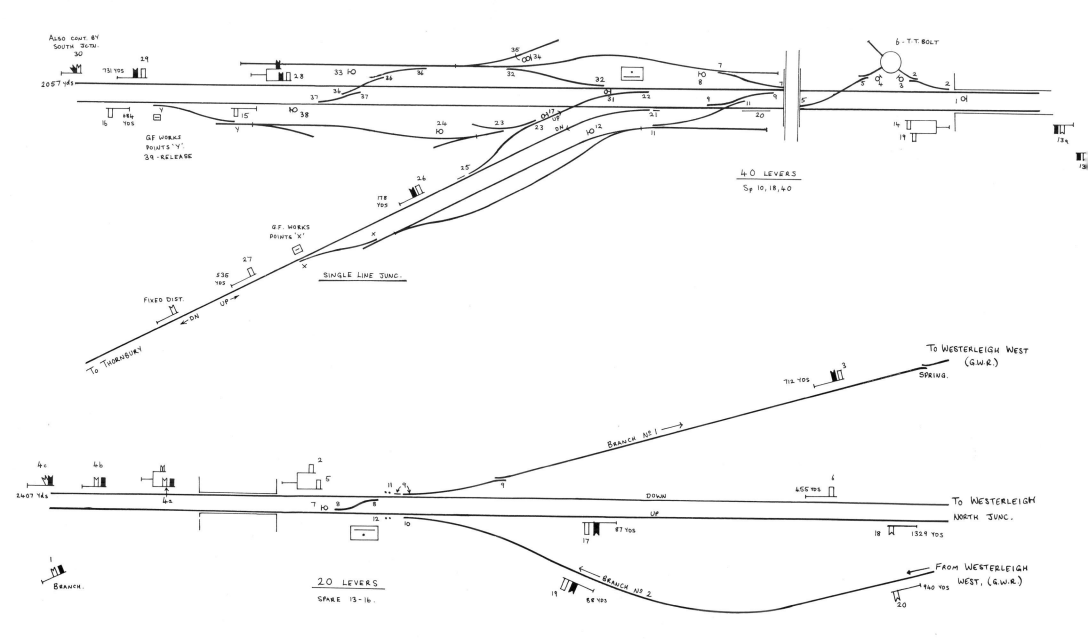

Also cont. by
South Jctn.
30

731 yds
29

2057 yds

35
34
33
32
32

28
36
36
36

37
37

31
22

7
8

7

6 - T.T. BOLT

5
4
3
2

2

1

16
684
yds
Y

15

38

Y

GF WORKS
POINTS 'Y'.
39 - RELEASE

24
23
23

17
UP

12
11

14
19

13a

13

21

21

20

11

9

9

5

40 LEVERS
Sp 10, 18, 40

25

26

178
YDS

G.F. WORKS
POINTS 'X'

X

27

535
YDS

X

SINGLE LINE JUNC.

FIXED DIST.

DN

UP

TO THORNBURY

TO WESTERLEIGH WEST
(G.W.R.)

712 YDS

3

SPRING.

BRANCH Nº 1

4c

4b

2
5

11
9

9

6

455 YDS

TO WESTERLEIGH

DOWN

2407 yds

4a

7
8
8

UP

NORTH JUNC.

17
87 YDS

18
1329 YDS

12

10

1

FROM WESTERLEIGH
WEST, (G.W.R.)

BRANCH.

20 LEVERS

SPARE 13-16.

19
BRANCH Nº 2
88 YDS

20
940 YDS

YATE No. 1 COLLIERY

The tiny coal pit called Yate No. 1 was at the northern edge of the North Bristol Coalfield, and was served by a line from the main line. It had closed by 1890, and little now remains at the site, although the line of the siding can still be seen.

EARTH SIDING

The 'Earth Siding' was at about 118m. 45ch., north of the colliery connection, on the 'up' side. It was used for the unloading of manure, presumably from the many shunting horses used in Bristol. Further details have not come to light, although, no doubt, luxuriant grass marks its site to this day!

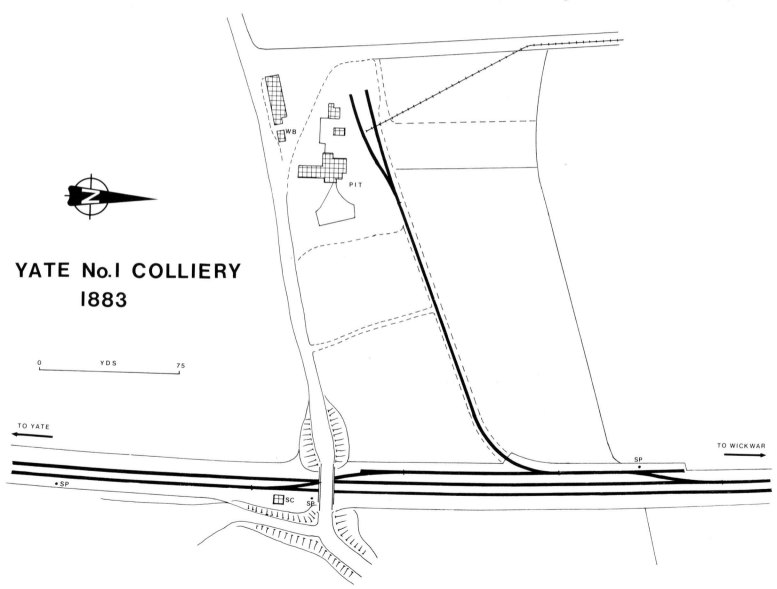

YATE No.1 COLLIERY
1883

0 YDS 75

TO YATE

TO WICKWAR

WICKWAR TUNNEL

The largest engineering work on the B&GR, Wickwar Tunnel, is 1,401yds. long, and has seven air shafts. The first trial bores were drilled in June 1840, and work began in earnest in April 1841. From the south, the tunnel passes through mountain limestone, so stable that it needed no lining; it then passes through sandstone, and finally Pennant stone, these latter requiring to be lined with 18in. thick brickwork. The toal cost of the tunnel was £43,994.

South of the tunnel, the line passes through a deep cutting cut into the limestone, crossed by a stream and a path on a narrow bridge. There is no portal at the southern end due to the stable nature of the rock.

Wickwar
The unique ex-LMS 'Jubilee' *Silver Jubilee*, just south of Wickwar Tunnel. The bridge carries a stream and a footpath.

L&GRP

Wickwar
LMS Compound No. 1057 bursts out of the tunnel with a local train for Bristol.

L&GRP

Wickwar Tunnel

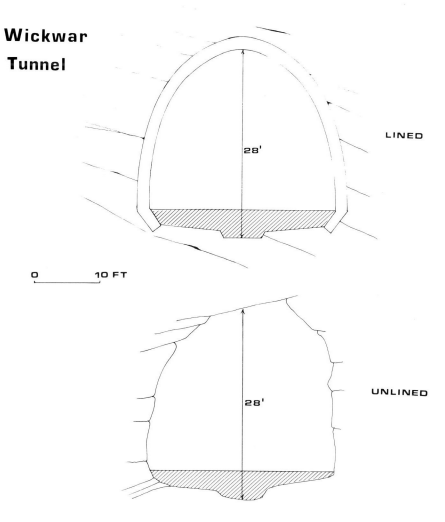

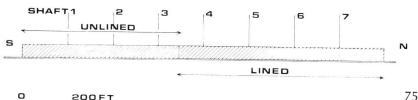

75

Wickwar
Track work in progress south of Wickwar Tunnel about 1890, emphasising what labour intensive work this was. The chairs are inside-keyed, with 45ft. rail lengths.

National Railway Museum

WICKWAR

Opened: Official, 6th July 1844; Public, 8th July 1844; Goods, 2nd September 1844
Closed: 4th January 1965

Wickwar Station was squeezed on to a very constricted site north of the tunnel. With two narrow platforms and a small goods yard it was convenient for the village, and also served the Wickwar Company's works. Due to the narrow site, the station building was at the top of a stone retaining wall, and had no canopy; very unusual for a Brunel design. The 'up' platform had only a tiny hut; again unusual as Brunel usually provided a matching shelter. From this, one can deduce that in 1844 this was the least important station on the line. The goods shed was of the standard design, and there was a small signal box opposite in a recess in the cutting side; this closed on 2nd November 1965. The sidings were taken out of use on 24th November 1963, and removed during the following February. The buildings have now been demolished, although part of the cider works remains, as does the retaining wall, and the station house as a private residence.

Wickwar
The station, circa 1910, showing the original shelter, which was a very poor structure. Note the non-standard nameboard, common to all the stations on the line.
Lens of Sutton

1932

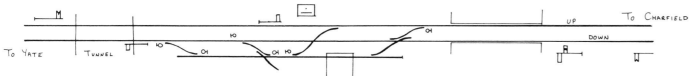

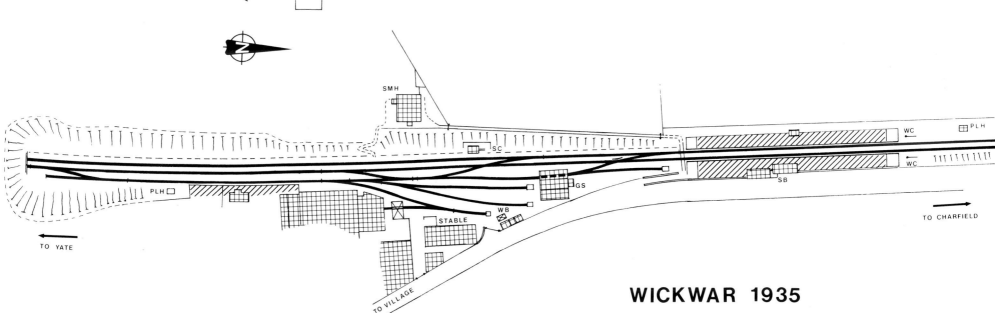

WICKWAR 1935

0   YDS   100

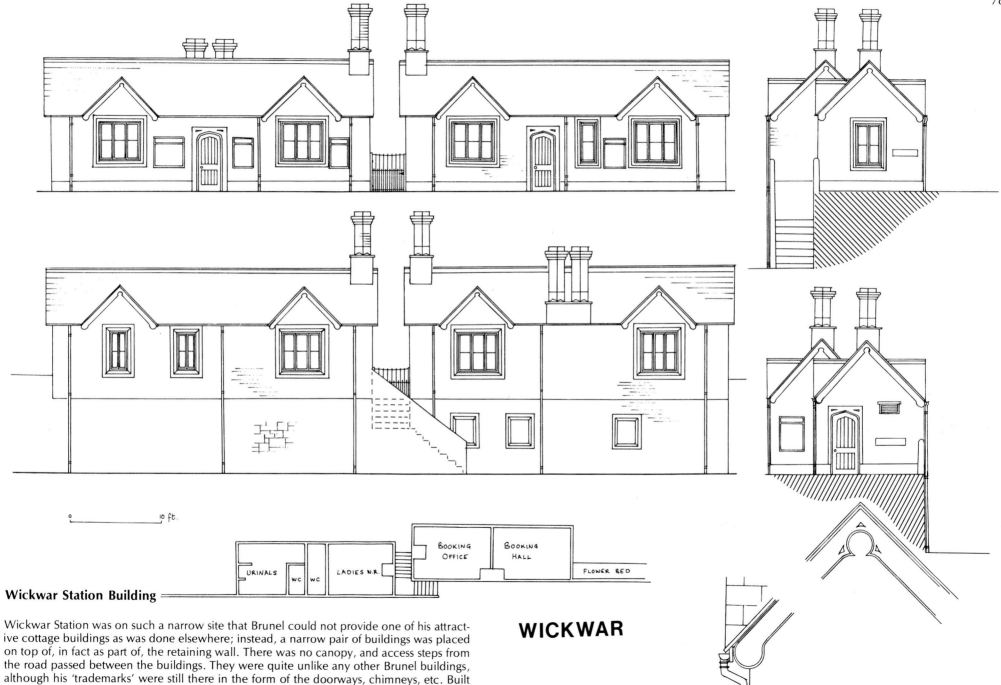

Wickwar Station Building

| URINALS | WC | WC | LADIES W.R. | | BOOKING OFFICE | BOOKING HALL | FLOWER BED |

WICKWAR

Wickwar Station was on such a narrow site that Brunel could not provide one of his attractive cottage buildings as was done elsewhere; instead, a narrow pair of buildings was placed on top of, in fact as part of, the retaining wall. There was no canopy, and access steps from the road passed between the buildings. They were quite unlike any other Brunel buildings, although his 'trademarks' were still there in the form of the doorways, chimneys, etc. Built in brick, with a slate roof, the building was demolished soon after closure in 1965.

Wickwar
Wickwar Station, quite unlike anything else designed by Brunel.

D. Ibbotson

Wickwar
The station staff pose on the platform, circa 1910.

Lens of Sutton

Wickwar
Wickwar, circa 1960; the 'up' platform shelter was an LMS replacement.

Lens of Sutton

Wickwar
An 'up' local train at Wickwar, circa 1950.

L&GRP

Wickwar
The goods yard, looking south.

D. Ibbotson

E.R.O. 30904
715 A
Please refer to

London Midland and Scottish Railway Company.
District Goods & Passenger Manager's Office,

R1/18582

In any reply.

_____ Bristol _____ Station,

April 21st 1932

In reply to your inquiry of ...., I beg to quote hereunder the present rates by Merchandise
Train between the Stations named.
They are quoted subject to the provisions of the Classification of Merchandise and the Conditions published in the Company's
Rate Books.
Messrs The Wickwar Quarries Ltd.,   Yours faithfully,

Charfield, Glos.   for G.S. Rider

From Chipping Sodbury to and	Description of Traffic.	Rate per ton and Conditions.
Wickwar (LMS)	Empty P.O. Wagons on own Wheels Exceeding 7 tons 5 cwts. and not exceeding 12 tons each in weight	Station to Station 11/9 per truck

PLEASE ORDER YOUR GOODS BY LONDON MIDLAND AND SCOTTISH ROUTE.

"C" denotes Collection, and "D" Delivery within usual limits. (Provided a Cartage Staff is kept at the Station for the purpose)
"S" denotes Station.   "P.S." denotes Private Siding.

NOTE.—Consignments not exceeding 3 cwt. in weight are subject to the Scales for Small Parcels, and Regulations for Small Parcels by Merchandise Trains contained in the
Classification of Merchandise. Consignments over 3 cwt. are charged not less than the charge for 3 cwt. at the Small Parcels Scales.
Rates quoted with the condition at "OWNERS RISK" are given on the terms that the consignor shall indicate to the Company when tendering the traffic that it is to be
carried at Owners Risk.

(2633)

Great Western Railway.
DISTRICT GOODS MANAGER'S OFFICE,
GOODS DEPARTMENT
BRISTOL. _____ STATION,
21/4/32 _____ 193

R6/72733.D.

DEAR SIRS,
I beg to hand you below the rate of conveyance by ordinary Goods train for the
Goods referred to in your enquiry of _____ hereon

The rates are quoted subject to alteration from time to time, and to the Company's
present and future Notices and Conditions of Carriage.
To Messrs The Wickwar Quarries Ltd.,   Yours faithfully,
WICKWAR.,   FOR F.W. TYLER

RATES for the undermentioned Goods, by ordinary Goods train subject to the
conditions herein specified, to the Regulations contained in the General Classification of
Merchandise, the additional charges in respect to heavy weights unless otherwise stated hereon,
and to the Conditions published in the Company's Rate Books.

FROM	TO	DISTANCE MILES	DESCRIPTION OF TRAFFIC.	RATES AND CONDITIONS. PER TON
Chipping Sodbury	Wickwar		Empty Wagons transferred for loading exceeding 7-tons 5-cwts each and not exceeding 10-tons each.	11/9d Per truck.

"C" denotes collection and "D" delivery within usual limits (provided a Cartage Staff is kept at the Station for the purpose).
"S" denotes Station, "P.S." Private Siding, "O.W." Owners' Wagons, and "C.W." Company's Wagons.
RATES quoted with the conditions "Owner's Risk" are given on the terms that the
Consignor shall indicate on the consignment note that the traffic is to be forwarded at
Owner's Risk.
NOTE.—Consignments not exceeding 3 cwt. in weight are subject to the Scale and Regulations for small parcels
by Merchandise Trains ; Consignments over 3 cwt. are charged not less than the charge for 3 cwt. at the Small
Parcel Scale.
PLEASE ORDER AND CONSIGN YOUR GOODS BY GREAT WESTERN ROUTE.
20,000- 8.31-(17)—P.O. S.

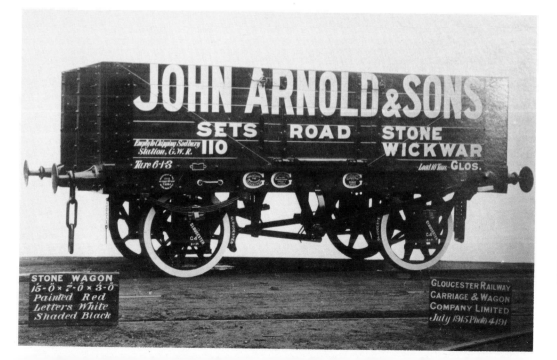

Wickwar
Date: 1915; Livery: Red, lettered white and shaded black. Registered with the Midland
Railway in 1915, although lettered to be returned to Chipping Sodbury (GWR)
OPC Collection

Opened: Official, 6th July 1844; Public, 8th July 1844; Goods 2nd September 1844

Charfield was opened with the B&GR in 1844, having the usual two platforms with Brunelian buildings in red brick. Between the platforms and the road bridge was the goods shed, with sidings radiating from a turntable. South of the station, a siding dating from 1846 served coal drops and there was a loading dock with a crane.

The buildings had the usual flat canopies, with stone decoration to the brickwork. The 'up' platform shelter was at some time altered by the MR, a glazed screen being added across the open waiting area, as was also done at Yate. The goods shed was less ornate than the others on the line, but built to the same basic design; the yard side was enclosed in 1847, and a house was built at the same time. In 1846, a Board meeting resolved to improve the water supply at Charfield, which led to the erection of a large water tower joined to the station house. There were water cranes at the end of each platform.

Charfield was originally worked from a signal box sited between the goods shed and the road bridge *(see Appendix)*; this was put in at the same time as the lay-by sidings to the north, in about 1875. This box closed on 1st August 1898, when the signalling was also renewed, two signal boxes being provided on the 'up' side of the line. On 29th July 1911, these were in turn replaced by a single box on the 'down' platform, this being the box which achieved notoriety in the Charfield disaster of 1928, when three trains piled up beneath the bridge *(see Bibliography)*.

The lay-by sidings were laid to allow goods trains to be overtaken, especially those travelling south, ascending Wickwar Bank. They were altered to loops in 1942, and a siding on the 'down' side served a brickworks, opened between 1882 and 1903, this being removed on 12th November 1961.

In 1956, the wagon turntable was removed and the shed road was realigned. Following closure of the station in 1965, the signal box closed on 16th May 1971, being removed for preservation in the Forest of Dean. At the time of writing, all other buildings remain other than the 'up' side shelter.

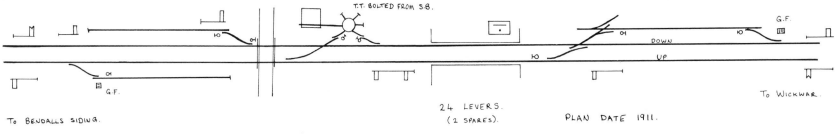

TO BENDALLS SIDING.

24 LEVERS. (2 SPARES).

PLAN DATE 1911.

To WICKWAR.

Charfield
The remaining buildings after closure.
J. Stephens

Charfield
The station in 1932. *L&GRP*

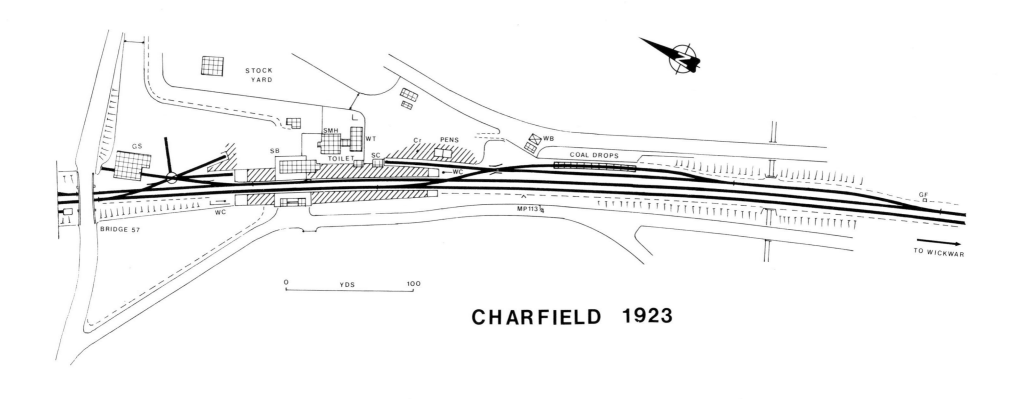

STOCK YARD

SMH WT
GS SB Cr PENS WB
TOILET SC COAL DROPS
WC
WC GF
BRIDGE 57 MP 113¾
TO WICKWAR

0 YDS 100

CHARFIELD 1923

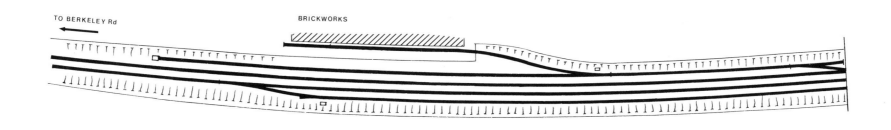

TO BERKELEY Rd   BRICKWORKS

Charfield
Ex-LMS 3F No. 43507 brings its train under the bridge and into the station, on 11th
May 1961.

C. Maggs

Charfield
The tender of ex-LMS 3F No. 43507 is topped up as it stands in the 'down' loop, north
of Charfield.

C. Maggs

Charfield
A view taken circa 1960, showing the simplified siding layout introduced by BR.

Lens of Sutton

Charfield
A view looking towards Wickwar.

Lens of Sutton

CHARFIELD

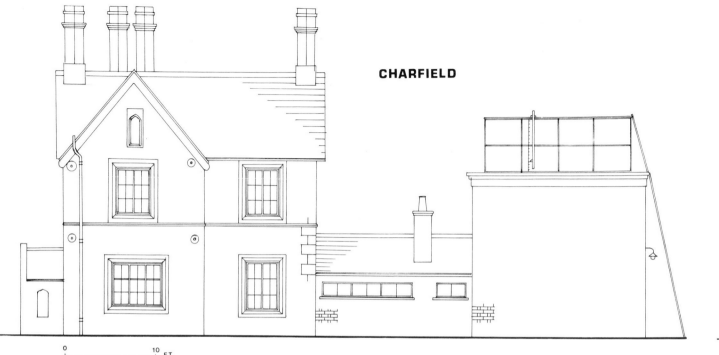

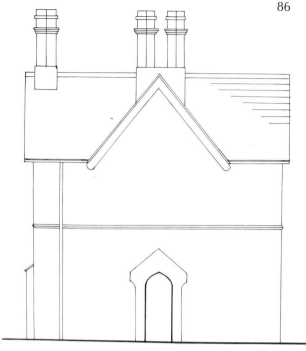

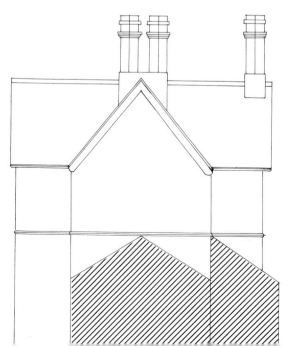

0   10 FT

Charfield Station House and Water Tank

One of the first things that the Midland Railway did when it took over the B&GR was to build a house at each station for the clerk, there being no stationmasters in those days. The house at Charfield was built in 1847 to this standard design, which blended in well with the Brunel buildings of the station, being built in local stone with a slate roof. At Charfield, the opportunity was taken to also build a water tank house, which was built in brick and attached to the station house. This must have been a very early example of a MR water tank, although the tank itself, which looked a standard MR item, may have been a replacement. It was built because of the station's position on Wickwar Bank, many goods trains running short of water by the time Charfield was reached. Both these buildings survive at the time of writing.

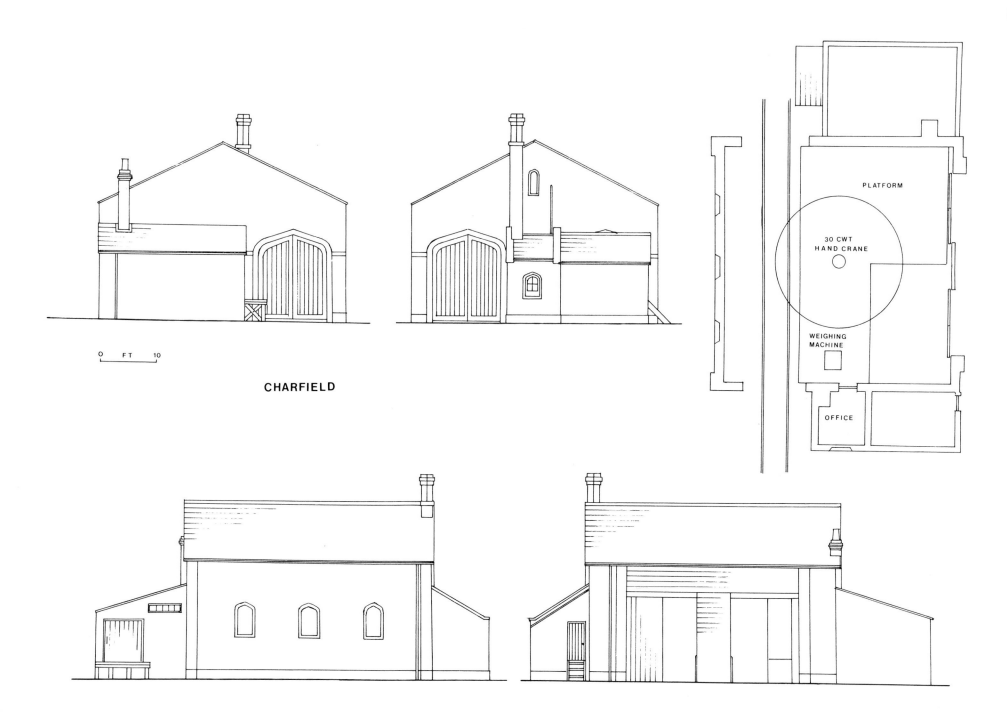

PLATFORM

30 CWT
HAND CRANE

WEIGHING
MACHINE

OFFICE

CHARFIELD

O   FT   10

BENDALL'S SIDING, HUNTINGFORD MILLING COMPANY

A mile north of Charfield, a siding on the 'up' side served a corn mill, owned by the Huntingford Milling Co., later Workmans Ltd. Laid in 1890 it had its own signal box, and served a shed on a platform, from which an elevated tramway ran to the mill. Most traffic consisted of box vans, one train a day shunting the siding in LMS days. The signal box had gone by 1922, the siding being released from Charfield. The same firm owned the mill at Draycott on the Dursley line, also rail connected, and they operated some private owner open wagons.

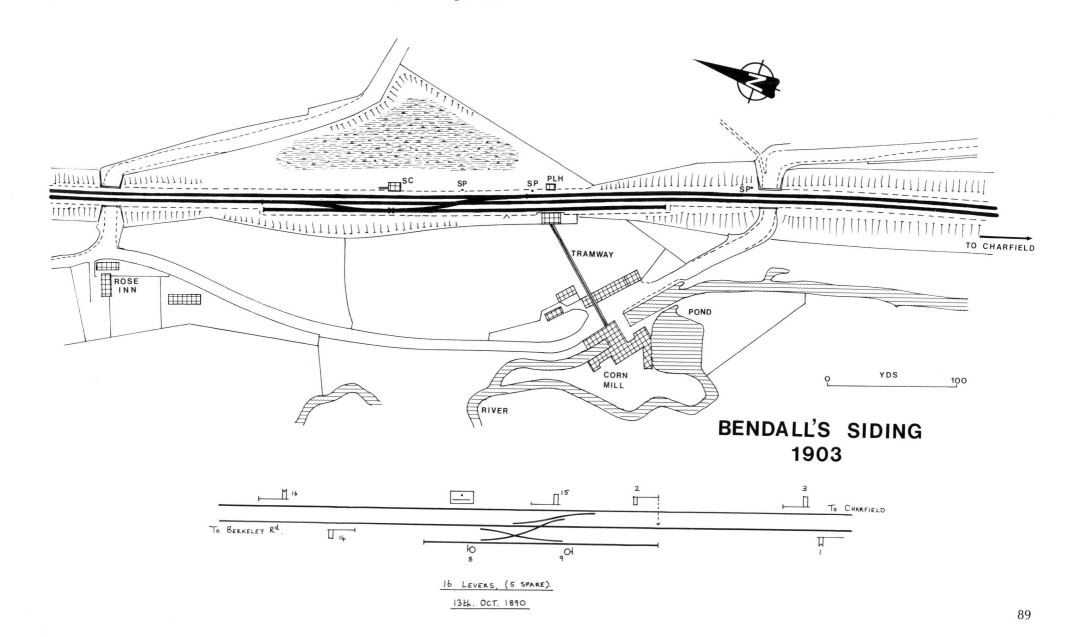

TO CHARFIELD

SC   SP   SP   PLH   SP

TRAMWAY

ROSE INN

POND

CORN MILL

RIVER

0   YDS   100

**BENDALL'S SIDING
1903**

To BERKELEY Rᵈ.   To CHARFIELD

16 LEVERS, (5 SPARE).

13th. OCT. 1890

BERKELEY ROAD SOUTH JUNCTION

Opened: 9th March 1908
Closed: January 1963

The junction at Berkeley Road South was put in by the GWR in 1908, to allow through running via the Severn Bridge when the Severn Tunnel was closed for maintenance, and to allow access to Sharpness Docks from the south. The junction was controlled from a MR signal box, but the loop line was GWR property. The MR used the loop line for a daily goods train from Sharpness to Bristol until 1945, when it was withdrawn, but GWR goods trains were more numerous, with many running at night. The only passenger trains to use the loop were diversions, frequently on Sundays. The signal box could be switched out when required. Closure of the junction was precipitated by the collapse of part of the Severn Bridge in 1960, when the loop line lost its main reason for existence, and it was little used thereafter until closure in 1963.

Berkeley Road South Junction
The view approaching the junction from the south, in 1953.
Dr A. Dickens

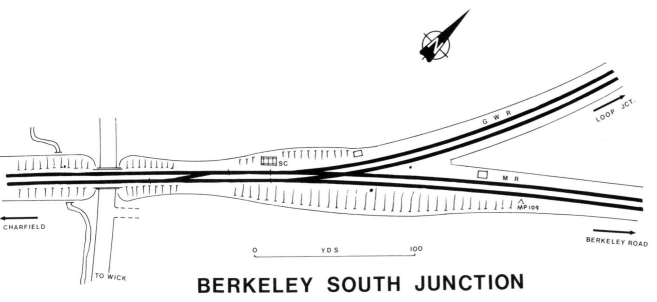

BERKELEY SOUTH JUNCTION

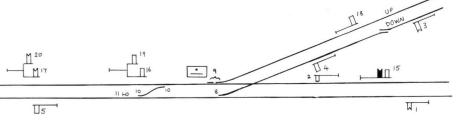

20 LEVERS

BERKELEY ROAD JUNCTION

Opened: (Station), 6th July 1844; Public, 8th July 1844,
                    Goods, 2nd September 1844
            (Branch) Passengers, 1st August 1876, Goods, 2nd August 1875
Closed: (Station) 4th January 1965
            (Branch) 2nd November 1964

Berkeley Road Station, one of the original B&GR stations, was some two miles from the village of Berkeley. First called Dursley & Berkeley, it was even further from the former place! Nevertheless, it was always a fairly busy station, having two platforms, on which stood the usual Brunel buildings. The goods shed stood on a loop siding, with a small cattle dock, and there was a stable for the horses used for shunting and for the local delivery drays. The station house was a large building, quite unlike any other on the line; it is the only surviving building. The station buildings were given wide canopies, later removed by BR, to the detriment of the buildings.

In 1875, a new branch was built to new docks opened at Sharpness where the

Gloucester to Berkeley canal met the River Severn and, a year later, passenger services began. The platforms at Berkeley Road were extended, and a new wooden station building was built between the converging lines. A footbridge was erected soon afterwards, the junction being controlled from a signal box.

The branch was absorbed into the Severn & Wye joint line, (MR&GWR), in 1894, giving the GWR access to the station, with little immediate effect. It was singled on 26th July 1931 and was increasingly worked by GWR stock, typically a 14XX or a pannier tank with 'B' set coaches, or a Hawksworth auto-trailer. Through working to Lydney ended in 1960, and the line closed to passengers on 2nd November 1964, although it remains open for dock traffic. The station closed on 4th January 1965, the buildings quickly being demolished. The signal box closed on 14th October 1968, the junction having been realigned on 2nd May 1965.

Berkeley Road
Berkeley Road, from the main line, circa 1880. Note the original signal box, slotted post signals, extended 'up' platform, and inside keyed track.

National Railway Museum

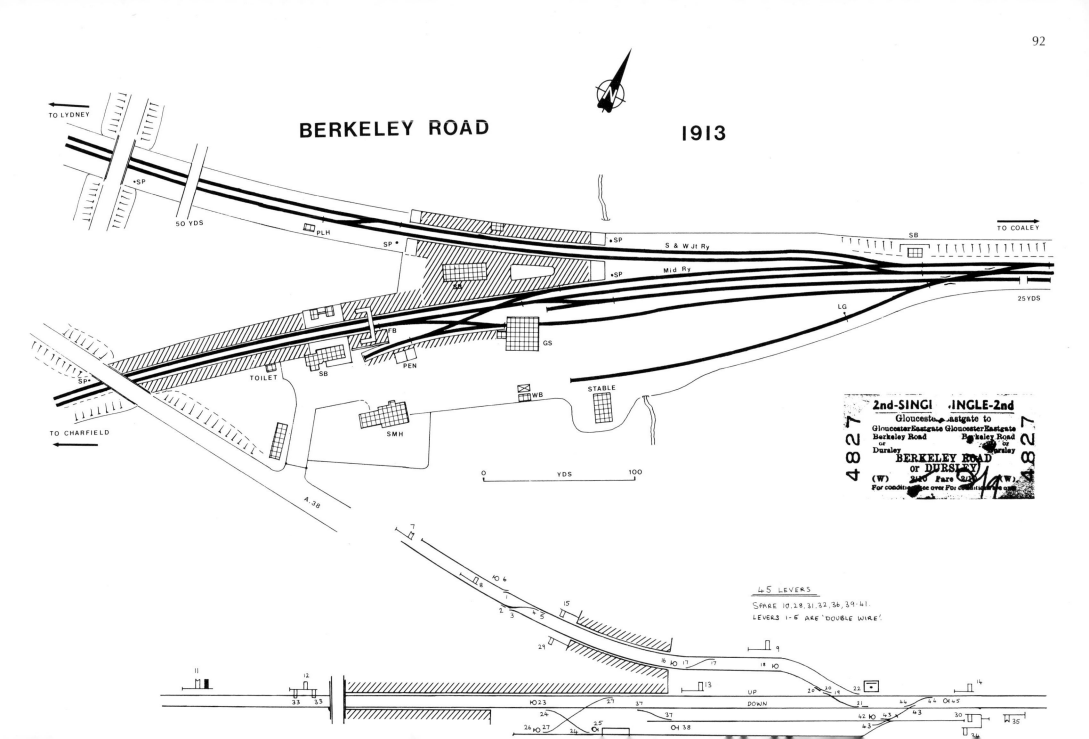

BERKELEY ROAD

1913

TO LYDNEY

50 YDS

TO COALEY

S & W Jt Ry

Mid Ry

25 YDS

PLH

SP

SP

SP

FB

GS

LG

TOILET

SB

PEN

WB

STABLE

SMH

TO CHARFIELD

SP

A.38

0   YDS   100

45 LEVERS
SPARE 10,28,31,32,36,39-41.
LEVERS 1-5 ARE 'DOUBLE WIRE'.

2nd-SINGLE SINGLE-2nd
BERKELEY ROAD or DURSLEY

4827   4827

UP
DOWN

Berkeley Road
The original buildings, after removal of the canopies.

C. Maggs

Berkeley Road
The S&W branch platforms at Berkeley Road.

Lens of Sutton

Berkeley Road
Ex-LMS Compound No. 41123 coasts into Berkeley Road with a local train from Gloucester.

H. C. Casserley

Berkeley Road
Ex-LMS 4F No. 44264 with a goods train from Sharpness.

C. Maggs

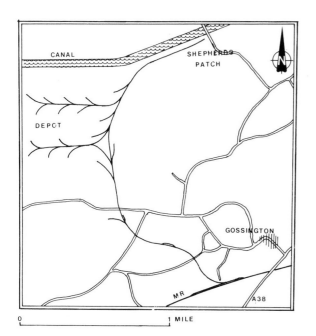

Opened: 1st July 1916
Closed: 1924

The sidings at Gossington were put in during 1916 to serve a huge munitions dump that had been established in the Vale of Berkeley. A branch ran from Gossington to the canal at Shepherd's Patch, and from this, ran a series of sidings serving the depot buildings, which covered a vast area. An engine shed was provided, which suggests that a locomotive was kept there permanently, but whether or not this was provided by the MR is not known. During the war years, the line must have been very busy, with trains running to the shell filling factory at Quedgely, near Gloucester but, by 1924, the depot had closed. The lines were removed on 21st February 1926 and the signal box closed. Little sign of the junction now remains.

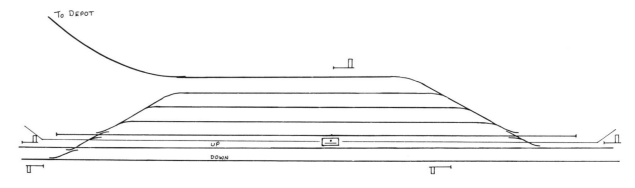

GOSSINGTON 1920

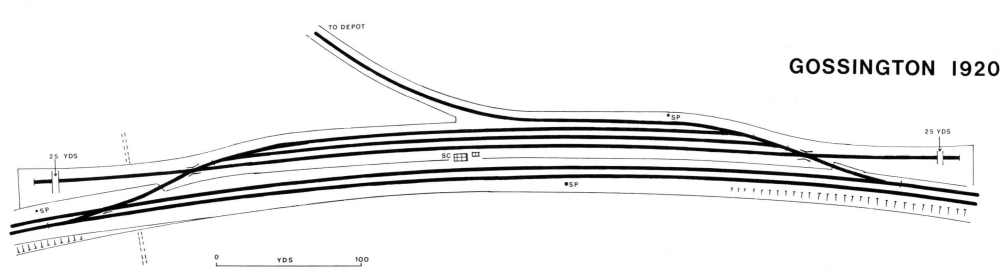

COALEY JUNCTION

Opened: Goods, 22nd August 1856; Passengers, 18th September 1856
Closed: Passengers, (Branch) 10th September 1962; (Main Line) 4th January 1965
Goods, 28th June 1968
Branch finally closed as a private siding on 13th July 1970

Coaley Junction, originally known as Dursley Road, was opened by the independent Dursley & Midland Junction Railway, who built the branch line to Dursley after the MR had refused to provide a station between Berkeley Road and Frocester. It was worked by the MR after 1861, and was later fully absorbed.

The station had two short main line platforms, with a very short and sharply curved platform for the branch train. Goods facilities were minimal, although there was a brick goods shed with an internal crane and loading platform. The signal box stood between the converging branch and main lines, the MR box being replaced by an LMS standard box on 31st March 1935. The station buildings were quite unlike anything else on the main line, or indeed on the MR, having been designed and built by the D&MJR. Built in red brick, with a steeply-pitched roof and ornate canopy, they were extended by BR in the 1950s. In the early 1930s, they were complemented by a tall monkey puzzle tree on the main platform!

The branch passenger service came to an end in 1962, although Coaley remained open until 1965, and goods trains ran to Dursley until 1970, by which time the line was a long private siding. The signal box closed on 14th October 1968. Only the goods shed and station house remain intact today.

Coaley
Coaley in 1932, with the branch of the left. A great deal of work has gone into the flower bed, with its monkey puzzle tree.   *L&GRP*

Coaley
The rear of the station building, showing the extension added by BR, circa 1952.
R. E. Toop

Coaley
The branch platform. Note the GWR signal post with LMS arms.
C. Maggs

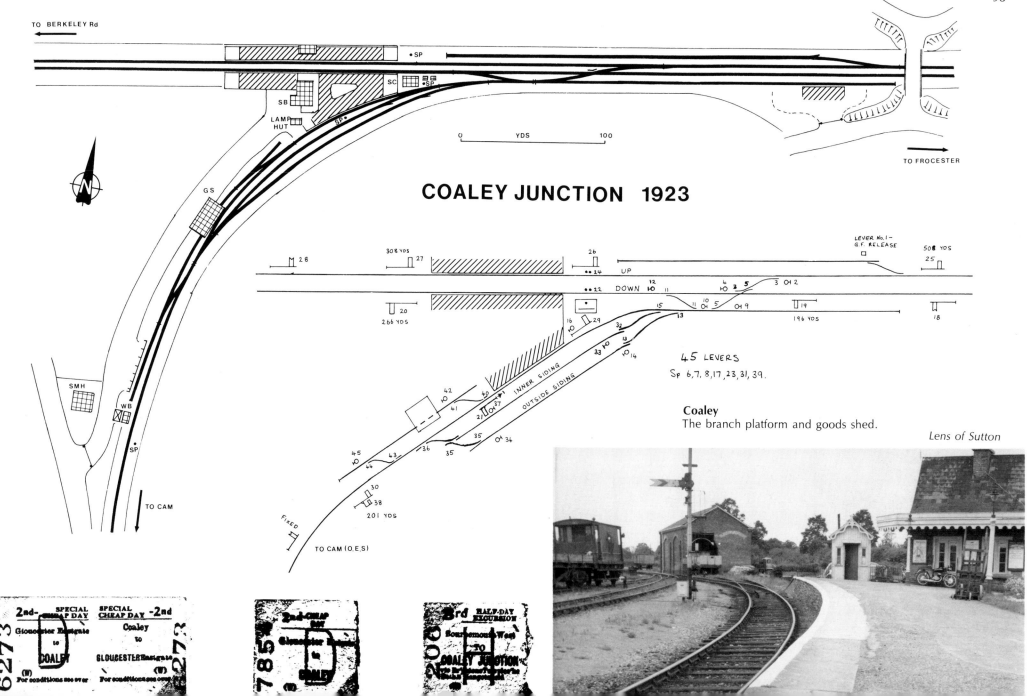

TO BERKELEY Rd

SP

SC

SB

LAMP HUT

SP

GS

0   YDS   100

TO FROCESTER

COALEY JUNCTION 1923

N

SMH

WB

SP

TO CAM

LEVER No.1 – G.F. RELEASE

508 YDS

28   308 YDS   26   25
        27   24   UP

20   22   DOWN   12   11   4 3 5   3   2
266 YDS   15   11 10 5   9   19
                              16 29   13   18
                                        32   196 YDS
                                    33   13
        42   39   33   14
                    41   37
                                    INNER SIDING
                            27   OUTSIDE SIDING
        45   43   36   35   34
            44
                    30
                38
        FIXED   201 YDS

45 LEVERS
Sp 6,7, 8,17,23,31, 39.

Coaley
The branch platform and goods shed.

Lens of Sutton

TO CAM (O.E.S)

Coaley

Unloading the parcels at Coaley, on 7th July 1962.

M. Mensing

Coaley

Grain hoppers for Draycott Mill are propelled up the branch by ex-LMS 0-6-0T No. 41720 past the coal siding and station approach.

C. Maggs

Coaley

The branch train at Coaley with ex-LMS 0-6-0T No. 41748, emphasising the sharp curve of the platform, on 22nd October 1955.

F. Shuttleworth

Coaley

Date: 1929; Livery: Black, lettered white and shaded red. There were two wagons, Nos. 11 and 12!

OPC Collection

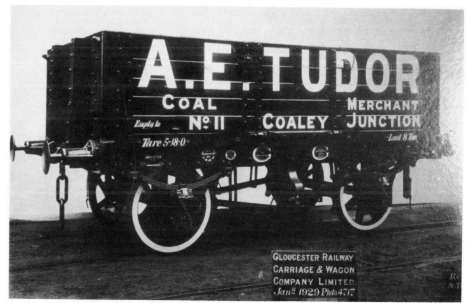

FROCESTER

Opened: Official, 6th July, 1844; Public, 8th July 1844; Goods, 2nd September 1844

Closed: 11th December 1961

The least used of the stations on the B&GR, Frocester, was an incredible survival from another age, with its Brunel buildings, wagon turntable, gaunt Gothic goods shed and short platforms. The track layout remained much as it was when built to the broad gauge in 1844. Fortunately, the original B&GR plan of the station has survived and is included here; note the short platforms, and the fact that the house has yet to be built. A refuge siding was added on the 'up' side in 1919, south of the station, but otherwise the layout remained almost unchanged, traffic never justifying any expansion, although the station was fairly convenient for the village, being approached through a lovely avenue of Beech trees.

The buildings were lovely examples of Brunel's art, until BR removed the canopies. Built in local stone, they were the smallest of Brunel's 'standard' designs, the station building being comparable with Culham or Minety & Ashton Keynes. Only the house remains today; also stone built, it cost £316 to build in 1847.

Frocester was staffed by a stationmaster and two porters; it closed before the other main line stations, in 1961. The sidings were removed in 1962, and on 11th May 1962, the signal box closed.

Frocester
The scene in 1932, before the canopies were removed, and with a local private owner wagon in the siding.

L&GRP

Frocester
Frocester, circa 1910.

Lens of Sutton

Frocester
The mutilated buildings, circa 1960.

C. Maggs

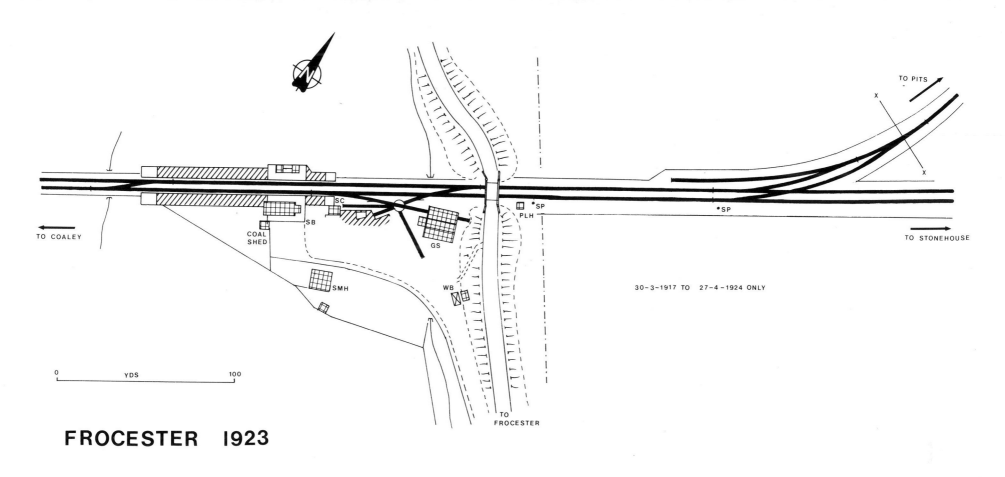

FROCESTER 1923

TO PITS

TO COALEY

TO STONEHOUSE

SC
SB
COAL SHED
GS
SMH
WB
PLH
• SP
• SP

30-3-1917 TO 27-4-1924 ONLY

TO FROCESTER

0   YDS   100

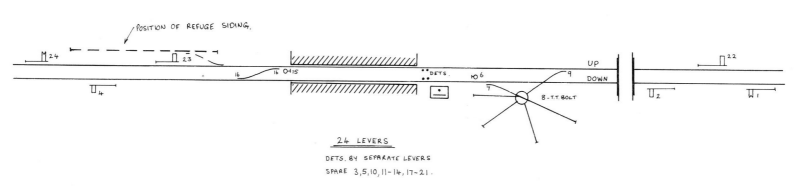

POSITION OF REFUGE SIDING.

24   23   22

16   16 &15   DETS.   &6   9   UP   2   1

4   7   8 - T.T BOLT   DOWN

24 LEVERS

DETS. BY SEPARATE LEVERS

SPARE 3,5,10,11-14,17-21.

1844

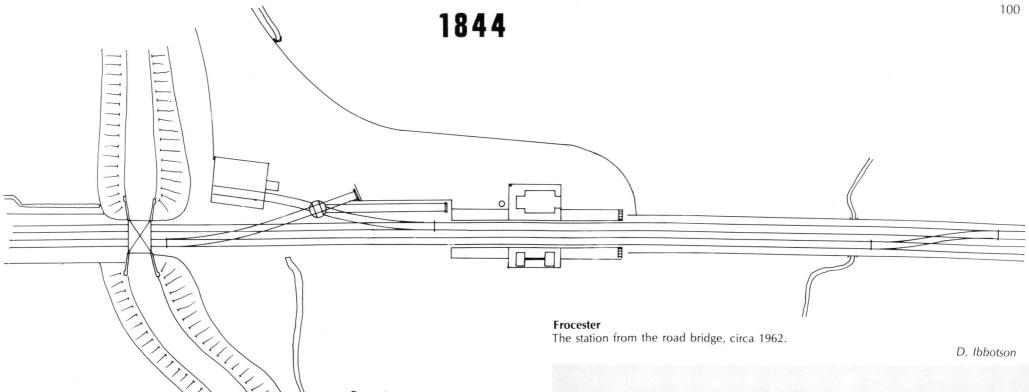

Frocester
Frocester goods shed and yard, circa 1962.

D. Ibbotson

Frocester
The station from the road bridge, circa 1962.

D. Ibbotson

Frocester

Frocester goods shed and yard, circa 1962. The shed remained open to the elements on the yard side, exactly as built in 1844.

D. Ibbotson

Frocester

The open side of Frocester goods shed, circa 1962.

D. Ibbotson

Frocester

Frocester Station was removed quickly after closure. This was the scene in 1964.

B. J. Ashworth

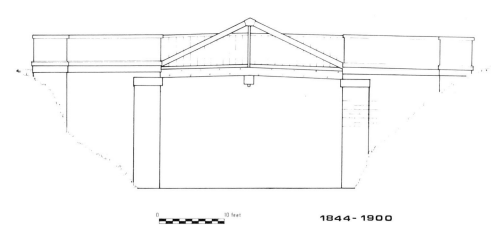

0   10 feet

1844 - 1900

FROCESTER

1900 →

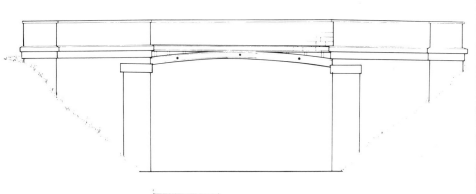

Frocester Road Bridge

When the B&GR was built, many of the minor bridges were built of wood, with stone or brick side walls, as was the one at Frocester which carried a narrow lane over the line. Two bridges were built to this rather odd design; one was at Fishponds Station, near Bristol and, I believe, this was the other, although it is not possible to be certain. The other type was much more often used for occupation bridges, etc. and lanes under the line. This bridge was rebuilt in 1900, according to a date on the side walls, and a metal span was put in, with stone parapets. This bridge remains in use today, and is seen in the photographs.

Frocester
Frocester goods shed and yard, circa 1962, showing the road bridge, as per the detailed plan, in the background.

D. Ibbotson

THE FROCESTER TO FRAMPTON BRANCH

During World War I, dock extensions at Avonmouth and London were using vast amounts of concrete, for which gravel was needed in large amounts. On 30th July 1917, a branch was opened from a junction just north of Frocester to gravel pits near Frampton-on-Severn, to help supply this need. The line was built as cheaply as possible, using German prisoner of war labour, with no significant earthworks. The junction ran directly into the main line, with marshalling sidings on the branch, where trains were sorted. Trains ran south, joining the GWR at Yate; two locomotives were used on the line, having spark arresting chimneys, and there was a large maintenance shed at Frampton.

The line was closed on 27th April 1924 and was quickly removed, the course reverting to agricultural use, although the pits, now flooded, remain.

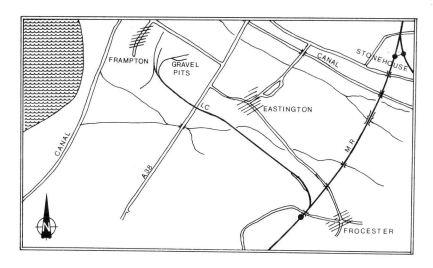

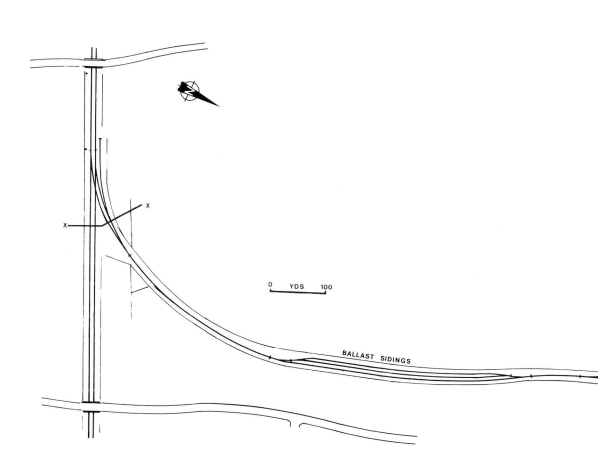

FRAMPTON BRANCH
1920

BALLAST SIDINGS

TO FRAMPTON

0   YDS   100

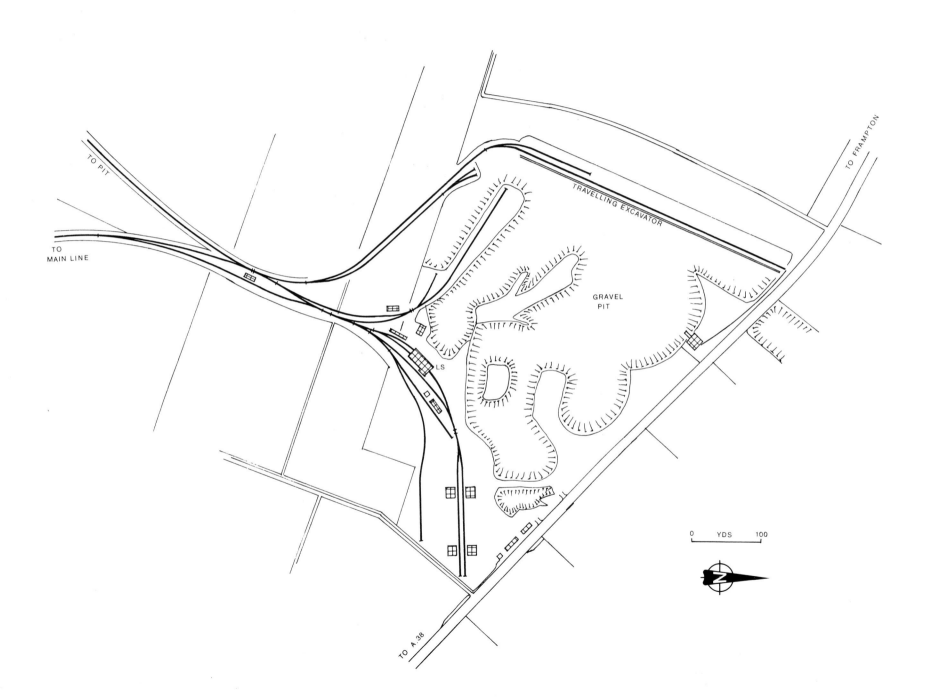

TO PIT

TO FRAMPTON

TO
MAIN LINE

TRAVELLING EXCAVATOR

GRAVEL
PIT

LS

TO A 38

0   YDS   100

N

STONEHOUSE VIADUCT

Also known as 'Beards Mill Viaduct', this structure was built for the opening of the B&GR in 1844, and as with all Brunel's structures at this time it was built of timber, as the drawings show. Rather flimsier than Brunel's later work in the West Country, it had ten spans of 50ft., with a partly-buried 20ft. span at each end. Carrying double broad gauge tracks, it was at most 43ft. tall.

In 1884, the MR decided to replace the viaduct with a more durable structure, as shown in the photographs . . . what a shame they did not also photograph the original! The new viaduct had metal lattice girders, resting on brick piers; the girders were replaced in the early 1970s. The embankment was extended slightly in 1884, and curved wing walls were built in brick. Just to the north, a similar bridge, now removed, crossed the Stroudwater Canal.

The MR used the viaduct as an excuse to obstruct the GWR in the 1920s; they refused to allow the use of GW 4-6-0 locomotives over it, as they had no 4-6-0s of their own, and thus had nothing to lose. The GWR had to carry on using the Churchward 'County' class 4-4-0 engines for longer than would otherwise have been the case.

Stonehouse Viaduct
Stonehouse Viaduct, when newly rebuilt in 1884. The date of construction is clearly visible in three places on the bridge and workmen pose for the picture in period costume.

National Railway Museum

106

1844-1884

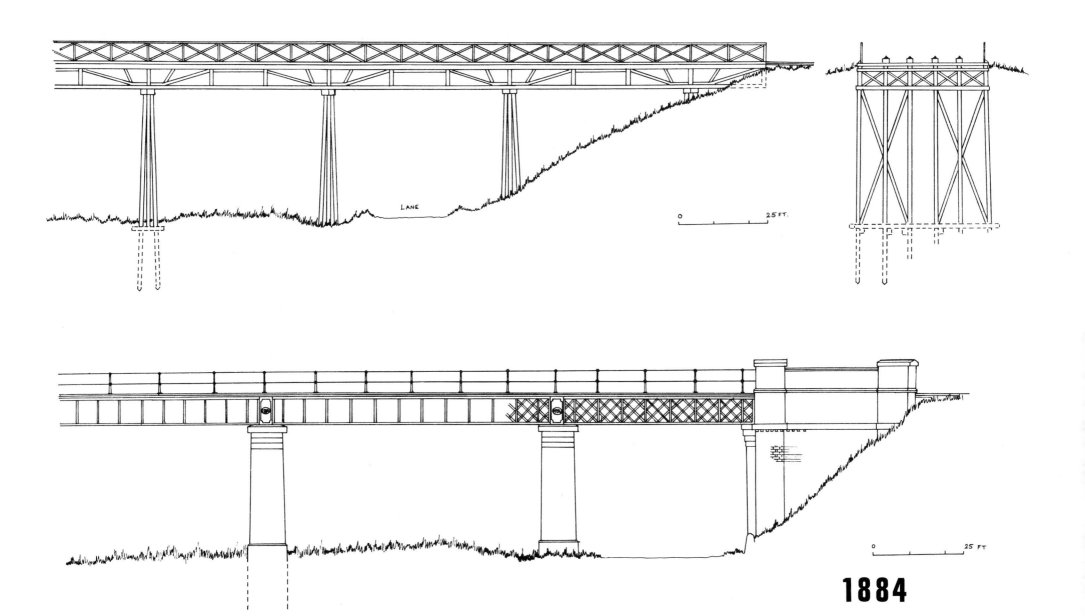

LANE

0   25 FT.

0   25 FT

1884

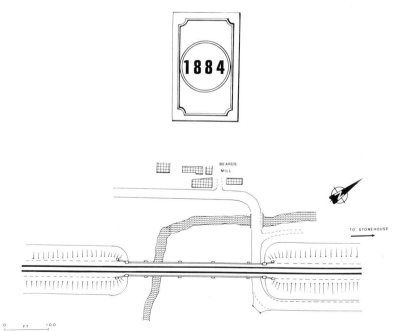

1884

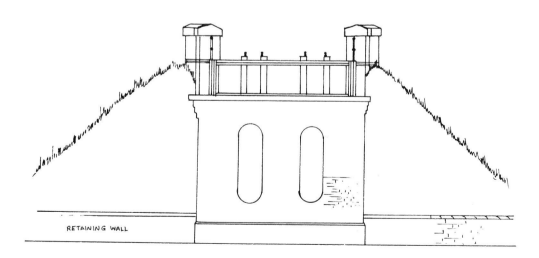

RETAINING WALL

Stonehouse Viaduct
A view of the complete viaduct in 1884, showing the final stages of construction.
National Railway Museum

STONEHOUSE

Opened: (Station) Official, 6th July 1844; Public, 8th July 1844; Goods, 2nd September 1844

(Branch) Passengers and Goods, 1st February 1867

Closed: (Station) 4th January 1965

(Branch) Passengers, 8th June 1949 (see note on Nailsworth line)

Goods, 1st June 1966

Stonehouse was the most northerly station on the B&GR in 1844. At first a fairly small affair, it had two platforms with stone-built buildings, and a standard goods shed. On opening, the track layout was very similar to that at Berkeley Road.

In 1867 the station became the junction for Nailsworth, but the branch was given its own platform some way from the main station, the junction being to the north. When the branch opened, the MR rebuilt the main station, extending the station building and replacing the shelter on the 'up' platform. The goods shed was doubled in size, all the work being done in a style complementary to the original. A house had been built near the 'down' platform in 1847, again in stone. The track layout was developed, a turntable being provided, and the branch station had a wooden building. A path connected the two stations, running through a covered way with glazed sides.

A large signal box stood facing the main line, and a footbridge was provided over the main line, another crossing the tracks near the actual junction. North of this was Oldends Lane level crossing, at which a crossing cottage was built in 1846; this remaining today.

In MR days, the staff on the station consisted of a stationmaster, two clerks, three loading porters, (plus a night shift), two guards, a yard foreman, two porters and a drayman. On 21st January 1934, the turntable was removed, most trains having tank locomotives. On the 'up' side of the main line, a siding was opened on 6th February 1940 into Hoffman's ball bearing works.

Passenger traffic on the branch ceased as a temporary measure in June 1947, but it was never resumed, the closure becoming official on 8th June 1949. The branch closed to goods traffic on 4th January 1966, the main station having closed from 4th January 1965. The signal box closed on 14th October 1968. The buildings have now been demolished and the road bridge rebuilt. There is a coal depot in the former goods yard.

Stonehouse
A very early view of Stonehouse Station.

Lens of Sutton

Stonehouse
The Nailsworth branch goods in seen about to join the branch at Stonehouse on 11th May 1961.

C. Maggs

Stonehouse
Stonehouse Station in 1947, showing the original part of the station building on the left.
L&GRP

Stonehouse
A special train prepares to traverse the Nailsworth line in 1964. The view also shows the goods yard.

B. J. Ashworth

Stonehouse
An RCTS special at Stonehouse, on 21st July 1963. The connection to Hoffman's works is on the right.

D. Cross

Stonehouse
Stonehouse, circa 1960.

Lens of Sutton

Stonehouse Station Building

The station building, with which modern travellers became familiar, was only partly the original structure. Brunel provided a standard cottage building in 1844 but, at a later date, the MR rebuilt the building and totally replaced the 'up' platform shelter. This was presumably in 1867, when the S&N line opened, or possibly in 1886 for the Stroud branch. An upsurge in traffic was no doubt anticipated and the original building was extended in a complimentary style. How much of the Brunel building was removed is hard to say, but the remaining section looks too small to have been the whole building of 1844. Both parts of the building were stone-built with a slate roof, and the extension was far from obvious. We can only speculate as to what the original 'up' platform shelter was like, although it was probably similar to Frocester, etc. The station buildings were demolished in the 1970s.

STONEHOUSE

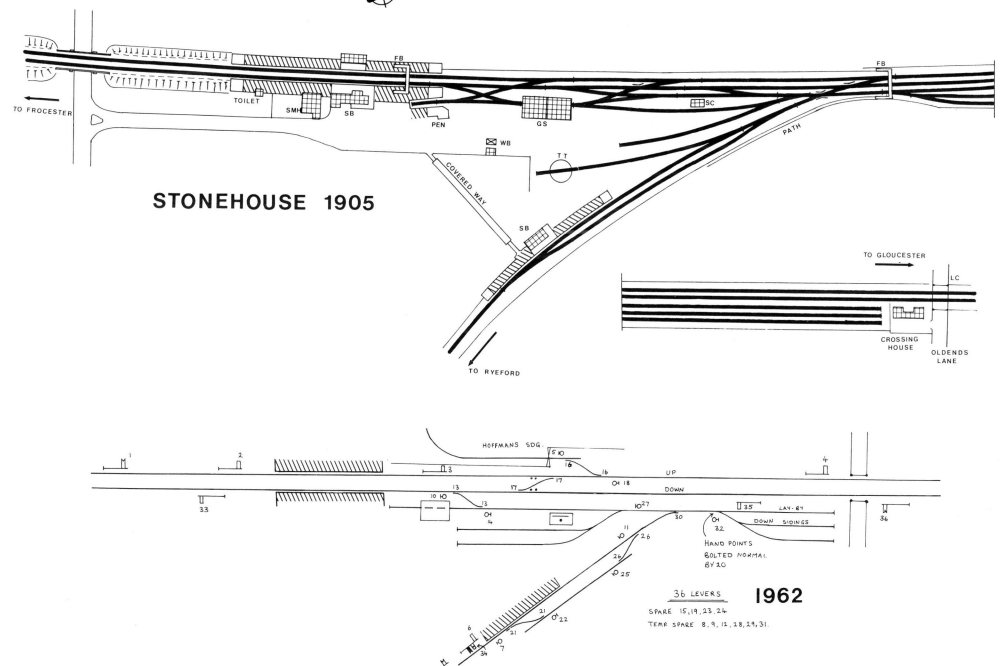

STONEHOUSE 1905

TO FROCESTER

TOILET

SMH

SB

PEN

FB

WB

COVERED WAY

SB

GS

SC

TT

PATH

FB

TO RYEFORD

TO GLOUCESTER

LC

CROSSING HOUSE

OLDENDS LANE

HOFFMANS SDG.

UP

DOWN

HAND POINTS
BOLTED NORMAL
BY 20

DOWN SIDINGS

LAY-BY

<u>36 LEVERS</u>
SPARE 15,19,23,24
TEMP SPARE 8,9,12,28,29,31.

1962

Stonehouse: Branch Platform Station Building

It would be reasonable to assume that this building was erected in 1867 by the S&NR for the opening of the Nailsworth line, but the building bears no resemblance to the other S&NR stations; rather, it reminds one of Stroud, which suggests that it was built by the MR when the Stroud line opened to passengers in 1886. What, if anything, existed before that, I do not know. The building was wooden, on a low stone base, and with a stone chimney, the roof being slated.

Stonehouse
The branch platform at Stonehouse in 1953.
Dr A. Dickens

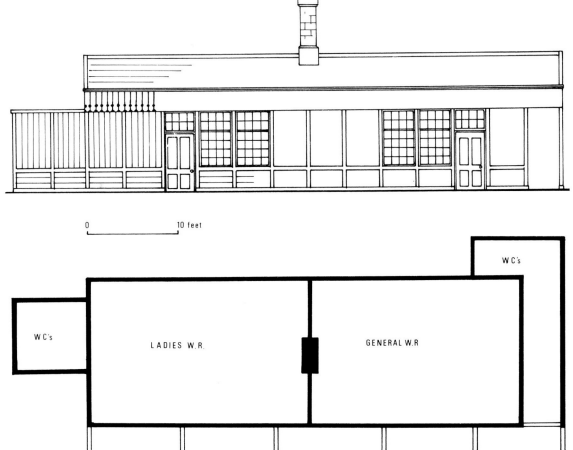

0   10 feet

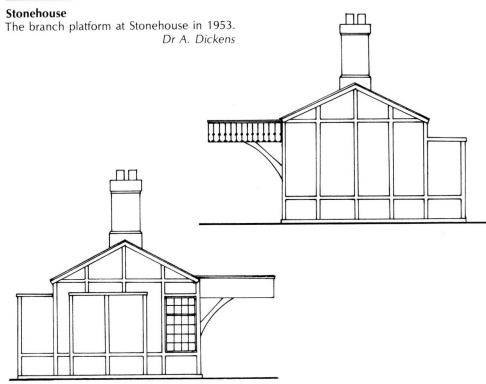

Stonehouse: Oldends Lane Crossing House

The crossing houses on the Birmingham to Bristol line were built by the MR in 1847 as single storey cottages, an upper floor being added at a later date. South of Gloucester, there was a similar building at Shortwood, south of Yate. The drawing shows a typical example, and is not of a specific building; for instance not all had the rear extension. The rear was blank, with no windows. The houses were brick-built, with slate roofs.

AS REBUILT

0   FT   10

AS BUILT

GROUND FLOOR

113

STANDISH JUNCTION

Standish Junction was where the Bristol & Gloucester Railway met the Cheltenham & GW Union Railway from Swindon. The two broad gauge lines shared the same tracks to Gloucester, but by the time the B&GR was opened, the C&GWUR had become part of the GWR.

On 29th May 1854, the MR opened its independent route into Gloucester alongside the GWR, so Standish ceased to be a junction from that date.

On 27th January 1873, a junction was re-established between the two routes, to allow the GWR trains to run south over the MR, the GWR having abolished the broad gauge in the Gloucester area in 1872. The running powers were only used for GWR goods trains. The MR built a signal box at the junction; a very early example of the MR signal box *(see Appendix)*.

In 1903, the junction was realigned for the start of GW passenger services over the route and a new signal box was built. GWR trains used the MR between Standish and Yate South Junction, where they joined the new GWR South Wales direct line into Bristol.

The expenses of the junction were shared between the two companies, including the signalman's wages . . . he in turn had to pass two lots of regulations! There were three shifts in the box and boys were employed to ease the work. At the height of the summer, in LMS days, there could be up to 80 trains to a shift.

For trains coming south on to the Bristol line, the rule was that the first train to pass Naas Crossing signal box would have precedence. There was naturally great rivalry, but the GWR often won, having larger goods locomotives for the most part. MR goods trains often ran short of steam on Wickwar Bank, causing a tail-back right to Gloucester, and once past Standish, there were no lay-by sidings until Charfield.

The GWR laid two loop sidings on the 'down' side of its line north of the junction, coming into use on 26th September 1943, and holding the equivalent of 77 wagons plus a brake van. Even this was sometimes found to be inadequate.

Standish Junction remains but, in 1968, the four lines to the north were reduced to two. The signal box closed on completion of the first stage of the Gloucester power signalling in 1968.

Standish Junction
A view looking north from the road bridge in 1932. Note the MR signals on the GWR line.

P. Copeland

Standish Junction
The junction in 1932.

P. Copeland

Standish Junction
The lines south of the junction in 1932, with the GWR climbing away on the left.

P. Copeland

STANDISH JUNCTION

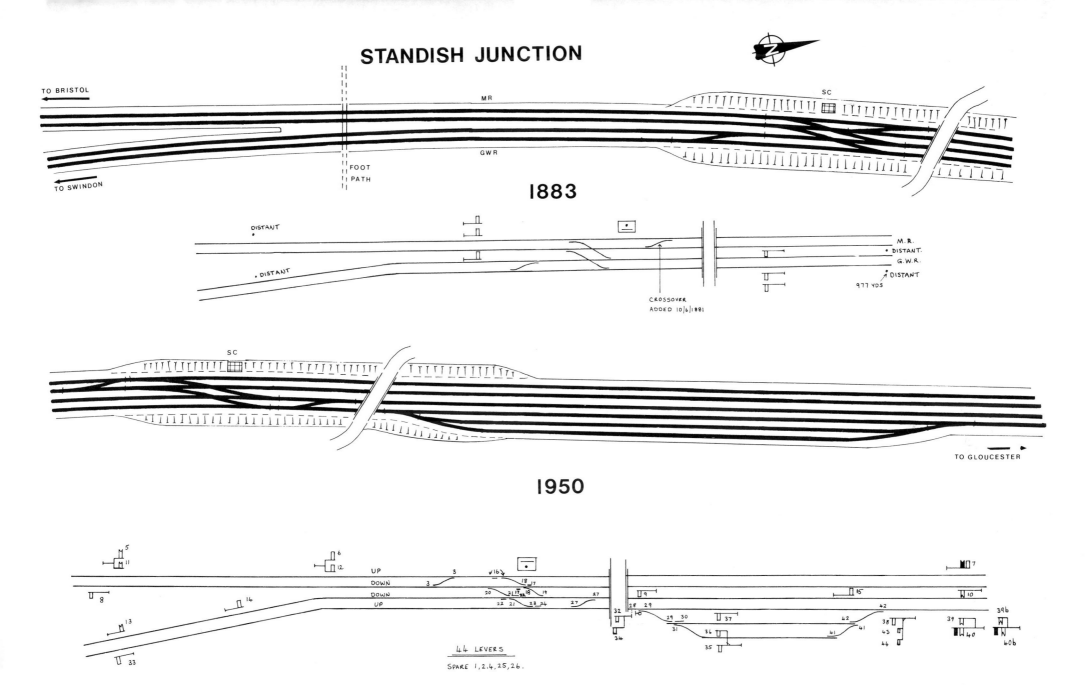

TO BRISTOL

MR

SC

GWR

FOOT
PATH

TO SWINDON

1883

DISTANT

M.R.

DISTANT.

G.W.R.

DISTANT

DISTANT

977 YDS

CROSSOVER
ADDED 10/6/1881

SC

TO GLOUCESTER

1950

UP
DOWN
DOWN
UP

44 LEVERS

SPARE 1,2,4,25,26.

Standish Junction
Ex-GWR 'Castle' No. 5063 *Earl Baldwin* at Standish on 20th July 1963.

H. Ballantyne

Standish Junction
A Paignton to Leeds express crosses on to the GWR at Standish on 20th July 1963, behind ex-LMS 'Black Five' No. 45253.

H. Ballantyne

Standish Junction
The junction as seen from the 'down' LMS line in 1932, showing the switched diamond crossing.

P. Copeland

HARESFIELD

Opened: 29th May 1854
Closed: 4th January 1965

Haresfield Station was opened by the MR together with the new standard gauge line between Standish Junction and Gloucester in 1854. The station originally had two wooden platforms, although the 'up' side was later rebuilt in brick, and a wooden station building was constructed on the 'up' side. A small signal box stood south of the level crossing. The 'down' platform was very narrow, and had no shelter, being squeezed in between the two main lines. A wooden screen protected waiting passengers from passing GWR trains.

The station would have been of more use had it been on the GWR line, as the Stroud Valley local trains could then have served it. As it was, a typical service was five 'up' and four 'down' trains daily, Haresfield had a stationmaster and two porters. The station closed in 1965, and was quickly removed to allow for realignment of the track.

I have been unable to find a scale plan or map of Haresfield, so the plan is lacking in detail, and is of only approximate accuracy; nevertheless it does give an idea of the station's layout. There were no points or sidings, and no goods facilities.

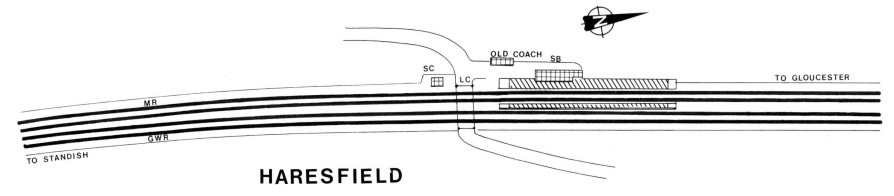

HARESFIELD

Haresfield
Haresfield, circa 1910.

Lens of Sutton

Haresfield
Haresfield in 1947, with an LMS 2P locomotive on a 'down' LMS train, and an LMS 4F on the GWR line.

L&GRP

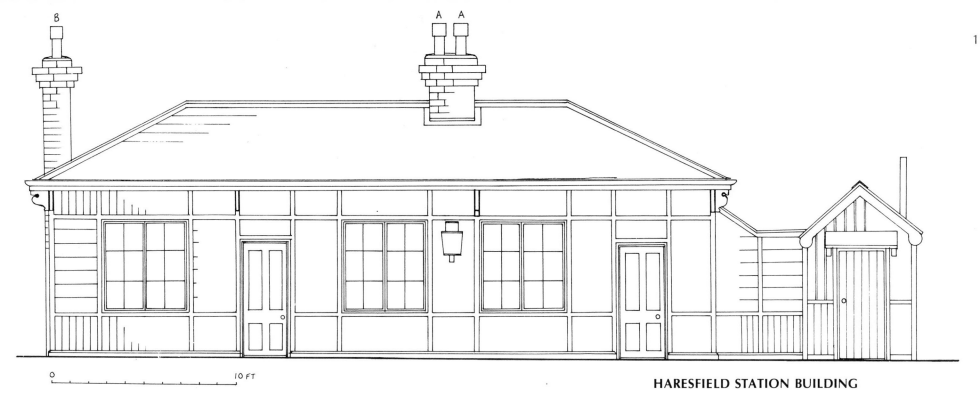

HARESFIELD STATION BUILDING

The wooden station building at Haresfield dated from the opening of the station in 1854. With a hipped slate-covered roof, the structure was all wooden, except for two brick chimneys. The small hut at the northern end appears to have been a lamp hut; this was shortened at some time, as shown. The building was demolished in 1965.

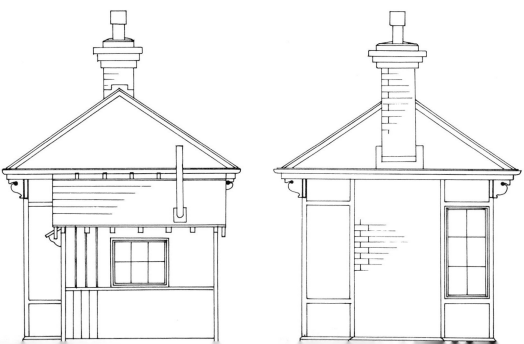

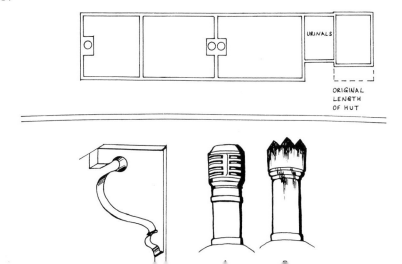

URINALS

ORIGINAL LENGTH OF HUT

0   10 FT

Haresfield
A local train arrives at Haresfield in 1964. Both platforms were originally wooden.
B. J. Ashworth

Haresfield
A local train, seen north of Haresfield behind LMS 2P 4-4-0 No. 528.

L&GRP

NAAS CROSSING AND QUEDGELY DEPOT

North of Haresfield was a small level crossing, Naas Crossing, with a small signal box on the 'up' side. In the 1880s, there was a trailing crossover north of the crossing.

Just to the north, at Quedgely, a shell filling factory was established, rail-connected, and it opened on 12th May 1916. There was a signal box, the factory being served by ammunition trains from the Gossington munitions depot, and trains of workers for whom a platform was built.

With the end of the war, the factory was run down, and the connections were removed in 1925 but, in World War II, the factory was re-established. This time the connection to the main line was at Naas Crossing, and controlled by the box there; the works remains today as a storage depot, still rail-connected. The signal box was replaced by a modern building in 1979 following a fire.

It has not been possible to include a scale plan of this location.

SECTION 3

THE NAILSWORTH AND STROUD BRANCHES

On 13th July 1863, an independent railway, the Stonehouse & Nailsworth Railway, was authorised to build a line from the MR main line to the Cotswold market town of Nailsworth, following the Frome Valley as far as Stroud. The line was built by the local company, with assistance from the Midland Railway, who worked in from the opening on 1st February 1867. There were no major earthworks, and stations were provided at Ryeford, Dudbridge (for Stroud), and Nailsworth. There were numerous sidings along the route serving cloth mills and other industries.

Woodchester Station was opened by the MR on take-over of the line in 1868, the original plan not having provided a station here due to the objections of some shareholders, who thought it would encourage use of a nearby Catholic convent. Amazingly, the Bill for the line had been defeated once for the same reason, when a station was proposed. The line was fully absorbed into the MR in 1878, having taken them that long to sort out the local company's finances!

It had been intended from the start to build a line from Dudbridge to Stroud, which it was expected would produce heavy traffic. It was left to the MR to build the line, which opened in November 1885 to goods, and on 2nd July 1886 for passengers. It saved the main branch, which had little traffic, and was worked as a separate line by the MR, Dudbridge becoming quite a busy junction.

The lines were destined to remain rather sleepy railway backwaters, but when the S&NR opened it had very big ideas, mainly promoted by the MR. The intention was to continue beyond Nailsworth, crossing the Cotswolds via Tetbury and Malmesbury, and eventually running to Southampton, giving the MR a route to the south coast, and cutting across the GWR heartland. Had the scheme come to fruition, the railway history of the area would have been very different, but the money ran out, and the line never got beyond Nailsworth. The terminus remained to remind travellers of the ill-fated scheme, with its odd track layout. The line would have been very expensive to build, needing steep gradients and heavy earthworks; perhaps there would have been a second 'Lickey Banker' shedded at Nailsworth!

The two branches were quite busy in the 19th century, with goods traffic always dominant, passenger trains being composed of four and six-wheeled coaches. Locomotives came from Gloucester Shed, Kirtley 0-6-0 and Johnson 0-4-4T engines being common. The latter type worked passenger trains up to withdrawal of the service. The lines were affected, early, by bus competition, and the GWR service from Stroud, and the passenger trains were suspended temporarily on 1st June 1947. They never resumed, and the closure was made official on 8th June 1949. Goods traffic remained important, and lasted until complete closure on 1st June 1966, by which time the trains were weekly, and the track became overgrown. The stations remained fairly complete into the 1970s, but now only Stroud and Nailsworth station buildings remain. The section from Stonehouse to Ryeford has been made into a cycle path and footpath, with further sections planned.

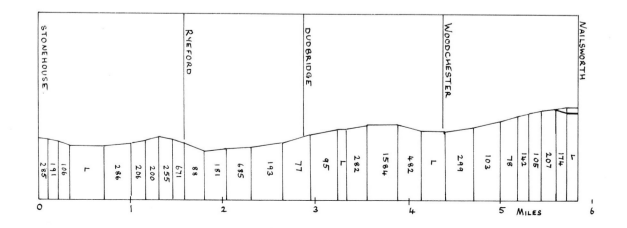
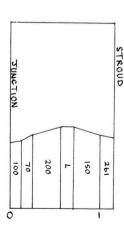

STONEHOUSE WHARF

When the Nailsworth line opened in 1867, a siding was put in next to the level crossing over the Stonehouse to King's Stanley road, serving a small wharf on the Stroudwater Canal. This section of canal remained open after the Thames & Severn section had closed, and the siding remained well into the 20th century, although latterly little used.

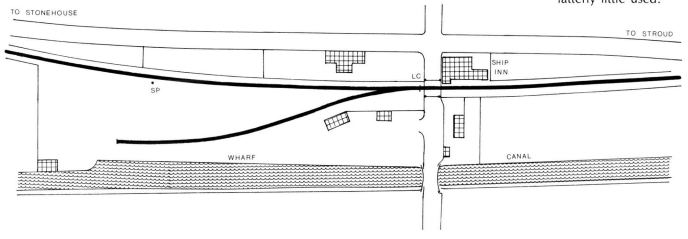

TO STONEHOUSE

TO STROUD

SHIP INN

LC

SP

WHARF

CANAL

STONEHOUSE WHARF 1908

0   YDS   100

Stonehouse Wharf
The site of the wharf in 1983.

Author

Stonehouse Wharf
The Ship Inn, with the site of the level crossing.

Author

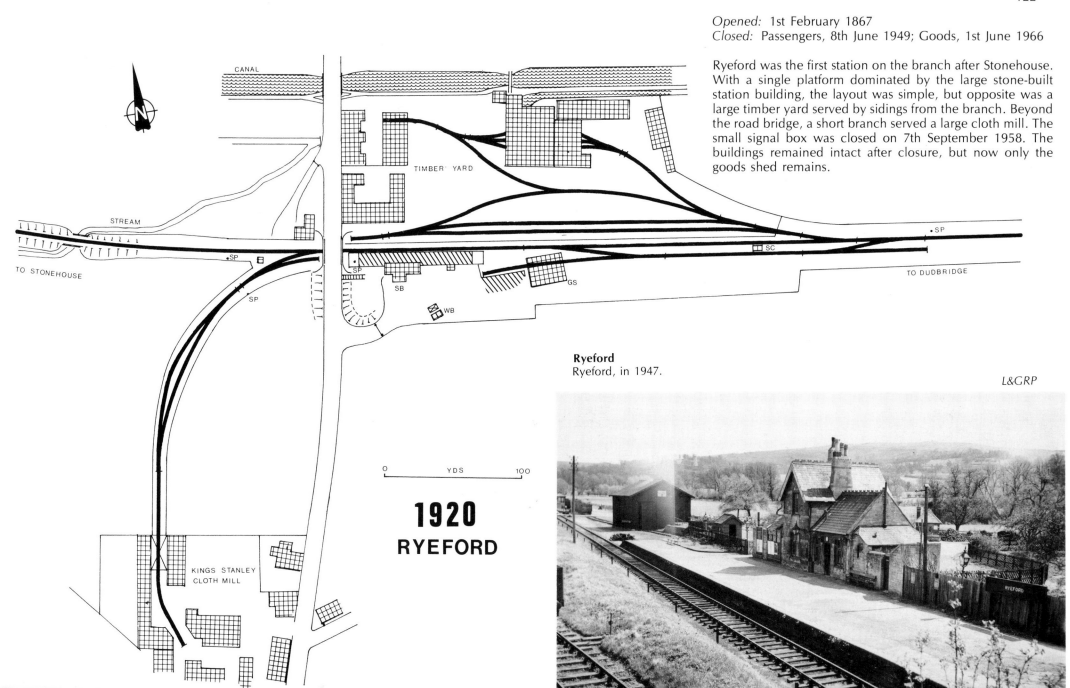

Opened: 1st February 1867
Closed: Passengers, 8th June 1949; Goods, 1st June 1966

Ryeford was the first station on the branch after Stonehouse. With a single platform dominated by the large stone-built station building, the layout was simple, but opposite was a large timber yard served by sidings from the branch. Beyond the road bridge, a short branch served a large cloth mill. The small signal box was closed on 7th September 1958. The buildings remained intact after closure, but now only the goods shed remains.

CANAL

TIMBER YARD

STREAM

TO STONEHOUSE

SP

SP

SB

WB

GS

SC

SP

TO DUDBRIDGE

0   YDS   100

1920
RYEFORD

KINGS STANLEY
CLOTH MILL

Ryeford
Ryeford, in 1947.

L&GRP

RYEFORD

Ryeford
Ryeford; the yard side.

J. Stephens

Ryeford
A goods for Nailsworth runs through Ryeford, circa 1956.

C. Maggs

Ryeford
The view from a special train on 25th August 1956.

H. C. Casserley

Ryeford
Date: 1907; Livery: Lead grey, lettered white and shaded black.

OPC Collection

LANES SIDING

This private siding served a rice meal mill owned by Lanes Ltd. After a period of disuse, it was removed, on 12th June 1933.

0 YDS 100

1920
LANES SIDING

TO STROUD

MEAL MILL

RIVER FROME

MILL POND

TO RYEFORD

•SP

•SP   GF

TO DUDBRIDGE

N

DUDBRIDGE

Opened: 1st February 1867
Closed: (Passengers) Actual, 1st June 1947: Official, 8th June 1949
(Goods) 1st June 1966

Dudbridge opened as the only passing station on the Nailsworth line, originally having a single platform with a large stone station building. A water tank stood on the 'up' side, behind which the land sloped up steeply.

On 16th November 1885, the short Stroud branch opened to goods, and to passengers on 2nd July 1886, and Dudbridge became a junction. A second platform was added and the goods yard extended, although there was never a goods shed, this traffic being dealt with at Stroud. The 'up' platform was cut into the hillside, backed by a stone retaining wall into which the waiting shelter was recessed. The actual junction was beyond the road bridge, and a seperate signal box was provided here. Both lines became single once the junction was passed, the Stroud line climbing away steeply.

In 1936, fares from Dudbridge included the following: to Bristol, 3/- (15p); to Birmingham, 7/11d (39½p); and to Gloucester, 1/- return (5p). The last station-master was Mr Kenneth O'Field, and he continued to live in the house for many years after closure of the line. Dudbridge Station signal box was made a ground frame in about 1927, the junction box surviving until 1966.

An oddity of Dudbridge was the small tramway which ran into the nearby mill across a trestle bridge, entering the mill at second floor level. The site of this can still be seen. The station site has now been cleared.

Dudbridge
Dudbridge Station in the 1950s.

C. Maggs

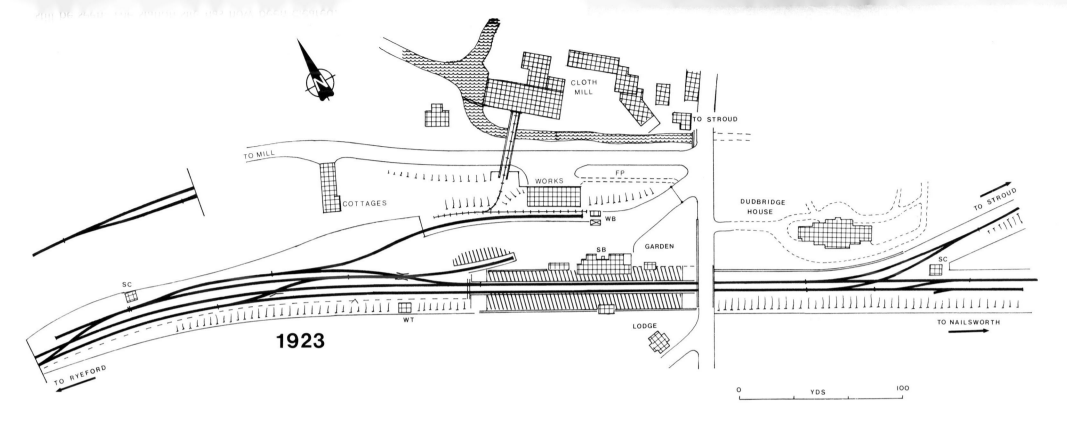

N

CLOTH MILL

TO STROUD

TO MILL

WORKS

FP

DUDBRIDGE HOUSE

TO STROUD

COTTAGES

WB

SC

GARDEN

SB

SC

SC

TO NAILSWORTH

WT

LODGE

1923

TO RYEFORD

0   YDS   100

DUDBRIDGE

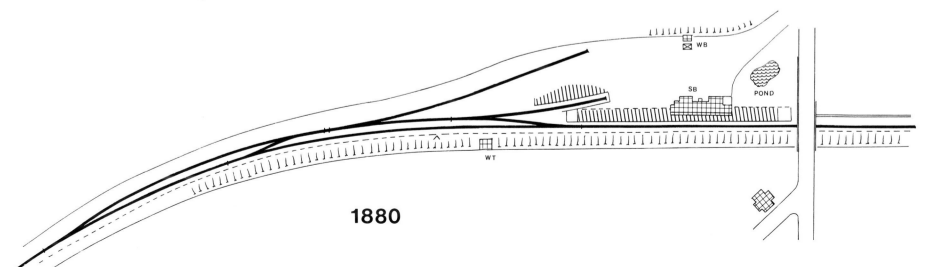

WB

SB

POND

WT

1880

Dudbridge Station Building

The station building at Dudbridge was built to the design of the Stonehouse & Nailsworth Railway in 1867. It made use of local Cotswold stone for the walls, and had a grey slate roof. The photographs show the building in LMS colours, probably brown and cream, as it was never repainted by BR. The building was demolished in the late 1970s.

DUDBRIDGE JUNCTION

126

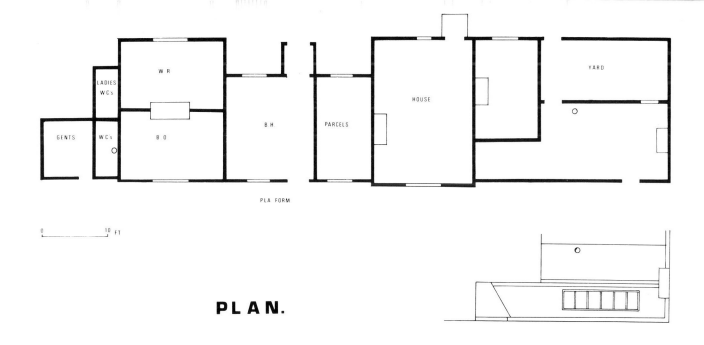

LADIES
WCs

W R

GENTS | WCs

B O

B H

PARCELS

HOUSE

YARD

PLA FORM

0   10 FT

PLAN.

Dudbridge
The yard side of the station building.

Dudbridge
Diesel-hydraulic locomotive No. D9521 shunts a few wagons on 4th March 1966.

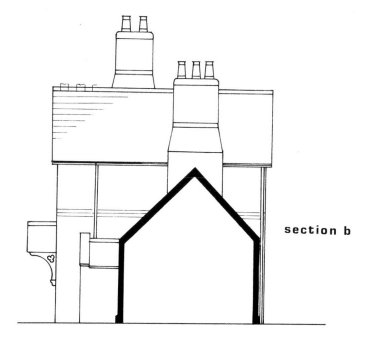

section b

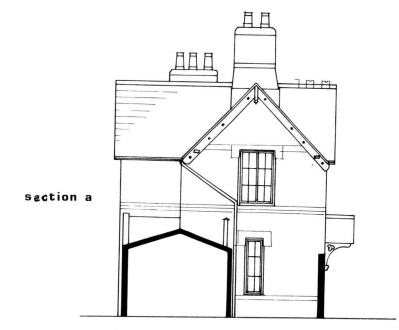

section a

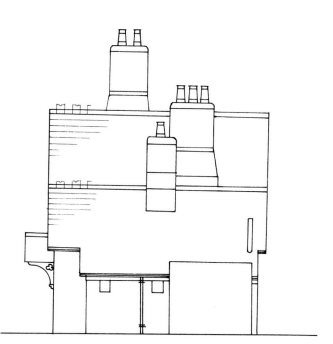

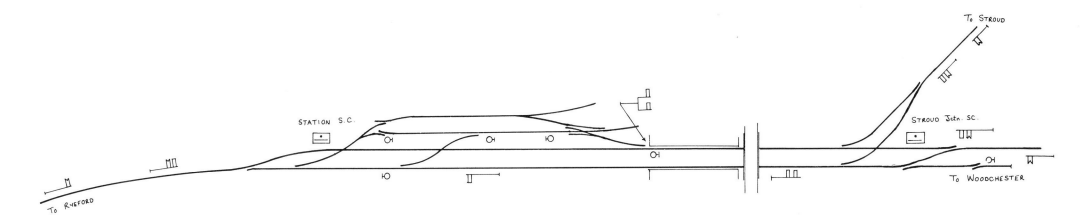

STATION S.C.

To STROUD

STROUD JCTN. S.C.

To RYEFORD

To WOODCHESTER

Dudbridge
The scene in 1960, with the loop lifted.

Lens of Sutton

Dudbridge
The 'down' platform at Dudbridge.

Lens of Sutton

Dudbridge
Ex-LMS 3F No. 43373 passes the junction with the goods for Nailsworth in 1955.
H. Ballantyne

Dudbridge
Ex-LMS 0-6-0 No. 43754 takes a shorter train up the branch to Stroud in 1956.
C. Maggs

Dudbridge
Date: 190?; Livery: Red, lettered white and shaded black.
OPC Collection

Dudbridge
The flour mill at Dudbridge; the tramway entered the door which is arrowed.
Author

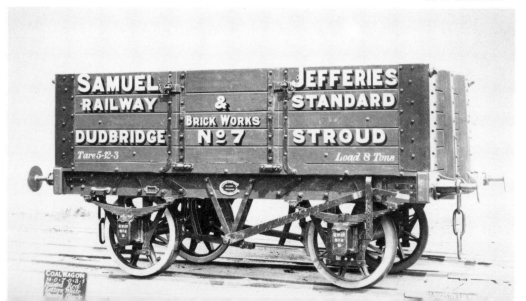

STROUD

Opened: Passengers, 2nd July 1866; Goods, 16th November 1885
Closed: Passengers, 8th June 1949; Goods, 1st June 1966

The steeply graded and sharply curved Stroud branch was opened in 1885, one of the shortest and most expensive lines per mile on the MR. The approach was across a double tracked viaduct of blue brick, and the station was on a huge embankment, built up alongside the Thames and Severn Canal wharves. The station had a long goods yard, preceded by a short platform with a large wooden building, a wide canopy covering the waiting area. The station was once famed for its flowers, but few people came to see them, as the GWR was nearer the town centre and more convenient for travel to London, Gloucester and the North.

Goods traffic was always more important, and continued until 1966. Surprisingly, most of the buildings remained intact . . . in 1886, the station building was described as temporary!

The siding shown dotted on the plan existed in 1900, but was lifted soon after. Between Stroud and the junction, a siding served Stroud gasworks, a small tramway taking coal from railway wagons to the works across a bridge. This was rope-worked, opening after 1902, and was derelict by the 1960s.

Stroud
Stroud Station, just before closure.

L&GRP

Stroud
A view looking towards the viaduct.

Lens of Sutton

Stroud
The rear of Stroud Station building in 1983.

Author

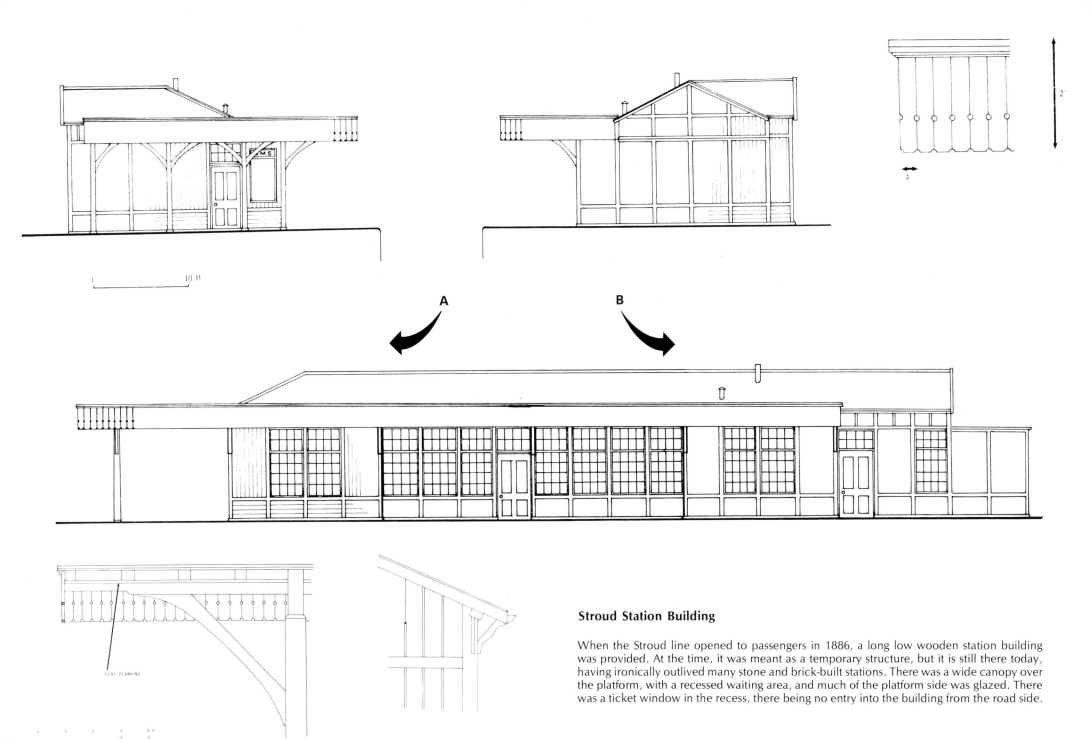

A

B

10 ft

FLAT PLANKING

Stroud Station Building

When the Stroud line opened to passengers in 1886, a long low wooden station building was provided. At the time, it was meant as a temporary structure, but it is still there today, having ironically outlived many stone and brick-built stations. There was a wide canopy over the platform, with a recessed waiting area, and much of the platform side was glazed. There was a ticket window in the recess, there being no entry into the building from the road side.

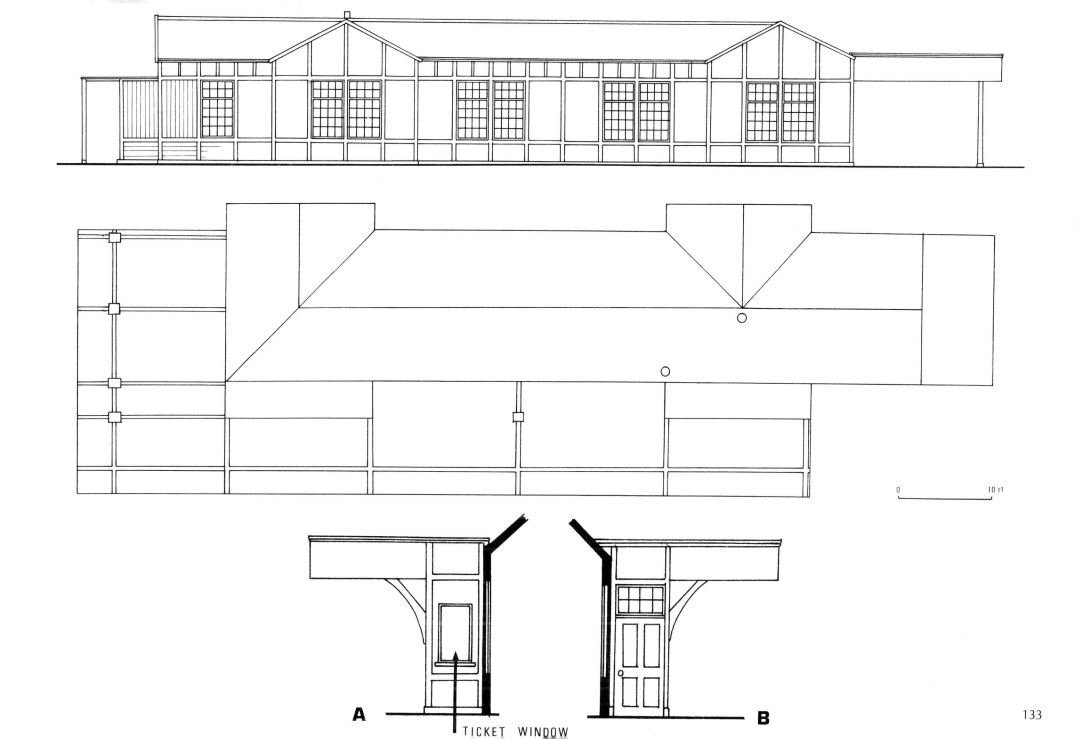

0   10 ft

A   **B**

TICKET WINDOW

133

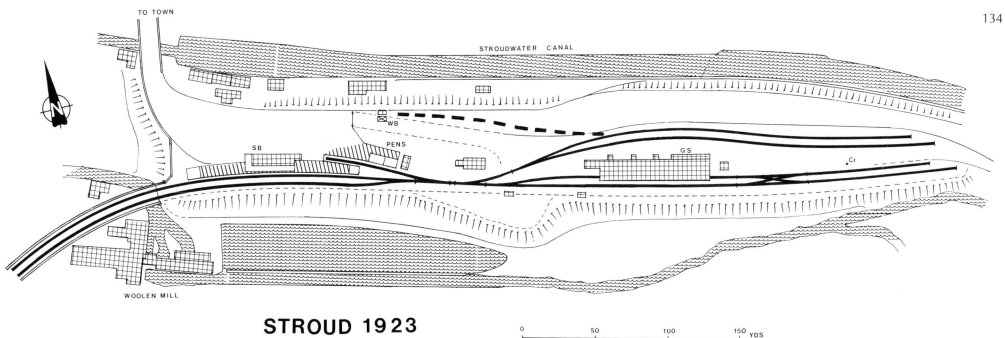

TO TOWN

STROUDWATER CANAL

WB

SB

PENS

GS

Cr

WOOLEN MILL

STROUD 1923

0   50   100   150 YDS

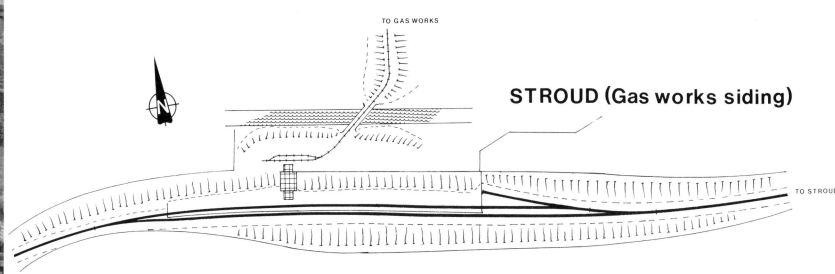

TO GAS WORKS

STROUD (Gas works siding)

TO STROUD

Stroud
The station approach road, crossing the canal, in 1983.

WOODCHESTER

Opened: 1868
Closed: Passengers, 8th June 1949; Goods, 1st June 1966

Woodchester was the only station on the line not to have an attractive stone station building. This, as already explained, was due to the fact that it was opened in 1868 by the MR. It was a poor affair, with small wooden buildings, a level crossing separating the platform and goods yard. Sidings from the yard served a large timber yard. The station had a small signal box by the crossing, but this had gone by 1949. Only the cottage by the level crossing remains today.

Woodchester
Woodchester in 1947, just before closure.

L&GRP

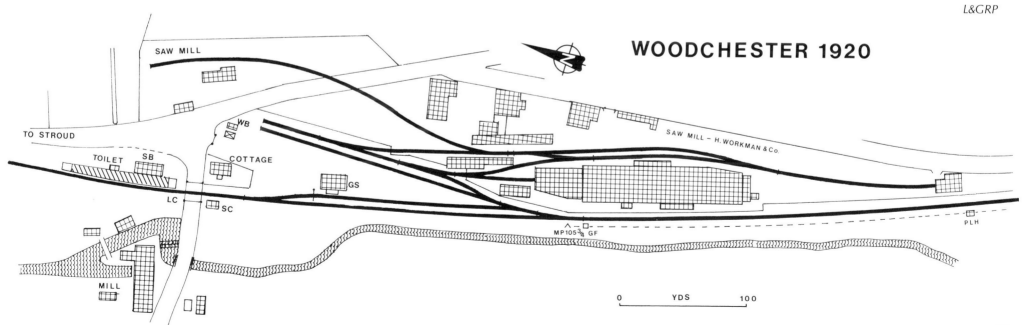

WOODCHESTER 1920

Woodchester
Woodchester Station in the 1950s, showing the crossing keeper's cottage; a standard
S&NR design also seen at Stonehouse Wharf.

C. Maggs

Woodchester
Woodchester Station on 31st May 1956. The ladder has not moved in nine years!

C. Maggs

Woodchester
Date: 1893; Livery; Black, lettered white.

OPC Collection

Woodchester
Livery: Lead grey, lettered white and shaded black.

OPC Collection

NAILSWORTH

Opened: 1st February 1867
Closed: Passengers, 8th June 1949; Goods, 1st June 1966

The terminus of the line, Nailsworth, was a station in two parts, with the passenger station at a higher level than the goods yard, which was nearer the town but approached by a steeply-graded line. The odd layout was a result of the original plan to extend the line.

The passenger station had a large stone building which dominated the short platform, again reflecting the desired main line status; in fact it always looked absurdly large. For the first few years, the Board meetings of the S&NR were held here, in what then became the booking hall.

There was a turntable near the platform, but this was out of use by 1930 due to the exclusive use of tank engines on passenger trains. The sidings here were removed in 1957.

The goods yard at one time housed a wooden engine shed, built in 1867, which was disused by November 1895, when the water tank and coal stage were moved to the position shown on the plan. The shed became derelict, and was demolished. There was a large brick goods shed, a cattle dock, and a large warehouse belonging to C. W. Jones & Co. stood near the entrance, as did some small wooden buildings owned by the same firm.

The station lines were removed in 1964, following the running of a railtour, having almost vanished in the grass. The goods yard was lifted in 1966. On my last visit, the warehouse and station building still stood, and the trackbed had mature trees growing in it. Nailsworth did have one claim to fame; I have never come across a small station at which so many private owner wagons were based. At least nine different firms based wagons there and several are illustrated.

Nailsworth
Kirtley 0-6-0 No. 2595 at Nailsworth, circa 1910.

Lens of Sutton

Nailsworth
Nailsworth, circa 1900, with an 0-4-4T engine on a train of six-wheeled coaches. Note the inside-keyed track.

Lens of Sutton

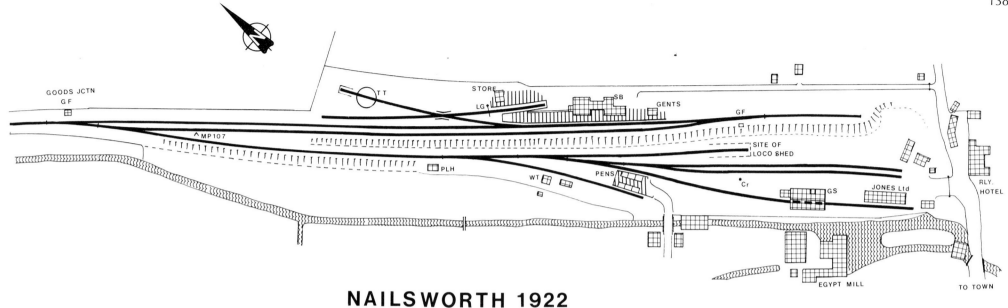

NAILSWORTH 1922

0   YDS

Nailsworth

Another view of Nailsworth Station, showing the ground frame, the point leading to the turn-table, and the large trees on the platform.

Lens of Sutton

Nailsworth

The branch goods is seen ready to leave. The Railway Hotel is behind the crane, with the goods shed far right.

C. Maggs

Nailsworth

Kirtley 0-6-0WT No. 2008 outside Nailsworth Shed in 1875. The platform line is behind the locomotive at a higher level.

Revd W. Awdry

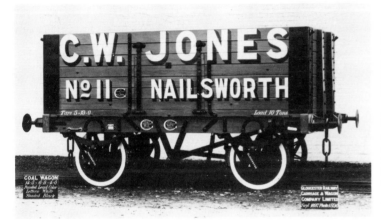

Nailsworth

Date: 1897; Livery: Lead grey, lettered white and shaded black.

OPC Collection

Nailsworth

Ex-LMS 3F No. 43754 takes water at Nailsworth.

C. Maggs

Nailsworth

(Left) Date: 1909; Livery: Chocolate brown, lettered white and shaded black.

OPC Collection

Nailsworth

(Right) Date: 1901; Livery: Purple brown, lettered white and shaded black.

OPC Collection

Nailsworth

Date: 1912; Livery: black, lettered white.

OPC Collection

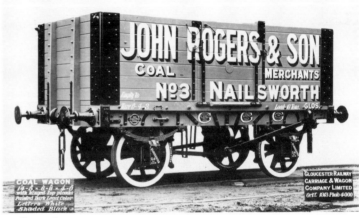

Nailsworth

Date: 1913; Livery: Lead grey, lettered white and shaded black.

OPC Collection

Nailsworth had a far larger building than a small branch terminus usually justified, reflecting the ambitions of the S&NR, who built it in 1867. The headquarters of the company, the stone-built building was entered through an arched portico, and glazed awnings covered a recessed waiting area. The large booking hall was possibly the original S&NR boardroom. On the northern end of the building was a station house, similar to that at Dudbridge and Ryeford. Happily, this attractive building survives today, following many years of disuse.

NAILSWORTH

0   10 FT.

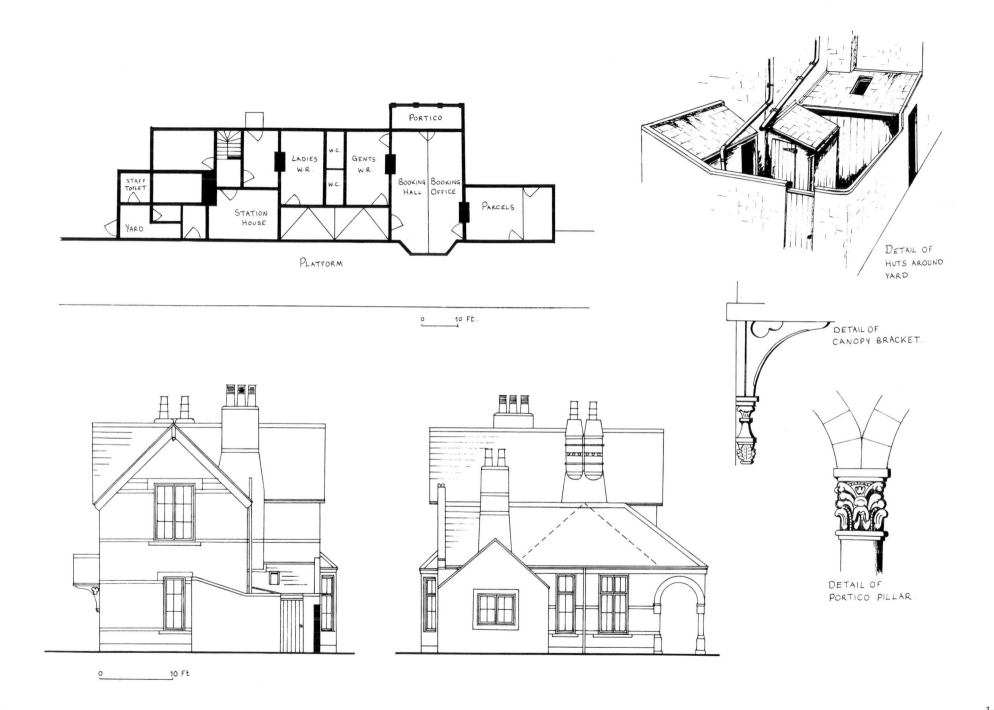

STAFF TOILET

YARD

STATION HOUSE

LADIES W.R.

W.C.

W.C.

GENTS W.R.

PORTICO

BOOKING HALL

BOOKING OFFICE

PARCELS

PLATFORM

0   10 FT.

0   10 Ft

DETAIL OF HUTS AROUND YARD.

DETAIL OF CANOPY BRACKET.

DETAIL OF PORTICO PILLAR.

141

SECTION 4

THE DURSLEY BRANCH

In 1846, the owners of the cloth mills in the Cam Valley, at Cam and Dursley, approached the MR with a request for a station at Cam Bridge, between Berkeley Road and Frocester. The MR, not unreasonably, refused, and the mill owners, along with other local worthies, decided to do the job themselves and build a branch line from the MR to Dursley.

The Dursley & Midland Junction Railway was opened for goods trains on 22nd August 1856, and to passengers on 18th September 1856, continuing as an independent line until 1861. Only 2¼ miles long, there were no engineering works of note, and only one intermediate station, at Cam. It was always a 'one engine in steam' line, without full signalling, although goods traffic was heavy, and a good passenger service was provided. The journey only took ten to twelve minutes, including the stop at Cam.

The MR worked the line from 1861, the D&MJR being wound up. A locomotive was provided from Gloucester Shed, which stayed at Dursley during the week.

The buildings on the line were distinctive, having been designed by the local company, and this included the main line junction, Coaley. All were built in red brick, except for wooden goods sheds at Cam and Dursley. In the 20th century, the line was worked mostly by Johnson 1F 0-6-0T engines, designed for goods work; regular performers were Nos. 1720, 1748, and 1742. The Johnson 1Fs lasted until 1956, when the WR introduced the 16XX class 0-6-0 pannier tanks to the line. The passenger service was withdrawn on 10th September 1962, goods trains running until 1968; the line remained as a siding to R. A. Lister's works until 1970. For a full history see *Bibliography*.

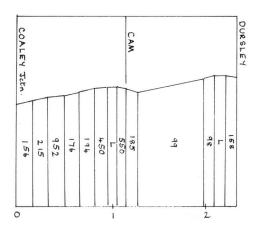

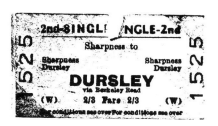

Cam
A train leaves for Coaley Junction on 1st October 1960.

H. C. Casserley

Cam
A Dursley train pases Cam Mill and milepost 107 behind 2-6-0 No. 46527 on 7th July 1962.
M. Mensing

These two sidings were situated between Coaley Junction and Cam stations, and served mills in the Cam Valley. No opening dates have been traced, although both existed in 1880. Nearest the junction was Draycott Mill Siding, serving a flour mill owned by the Huntingford Milling Co. The single siding was worked by a ground frame, the wagons being propelled to the mill from Coaley.

The other siding was to Middle Mill, latterly a board mill owned by Daniel & Co. Both sidings were closed in 1964, and the course of each can still be seen clearly.

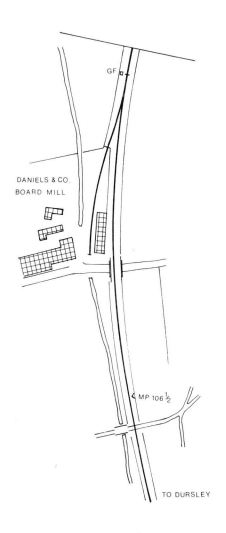

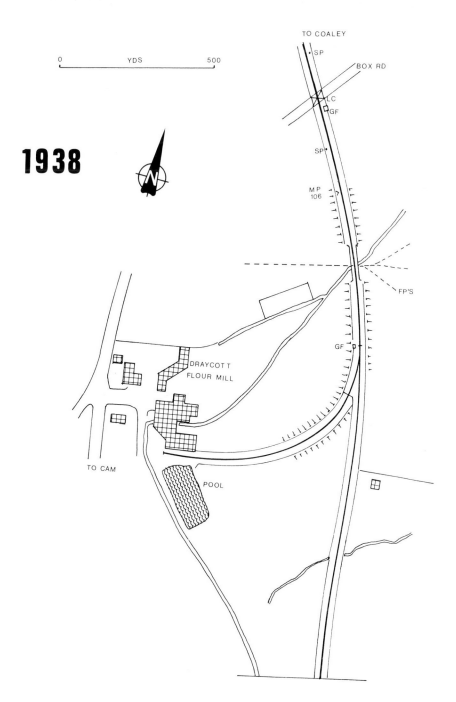

CAM

Opened: Goods, 22nd August 1856; Passengers, 18th September 1856
Closed: 10th September 1962

Cam was the only intermediate station on the line, and was situated conveniently for the rather spread-out village. There was a short single platform, on which stood a brick station building and a wooden goods shed. A level crossing at the platform end was worked by the station staff, the single goods siding being beyond the crossing.

The large cloth mill of Hunt & Winterbotham dominated the station, and was served by a siding, extended in 1916. In 1938, the LMS built a small ground frame hut from which the crossing was worked, and the station was signalled; there were five levers, operating the 'up' and 'down' home and distants, the centre lever locking the gates.

In later years, the station was run by one man, the porter's room being used by the permanent way gang. The station closed in 1962, and only the platform remains today.

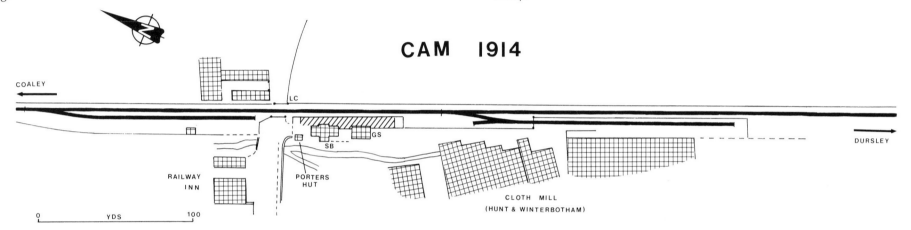

CAM 1914

Cam
Cam, circa 1960; note the short platform.

Author's Collection

Cam
Cam Station in 1932.

L&GRP

Cam
The level crossing and station entrance at Cam. The ground frame and signal date from 1938.
Author's Collection

 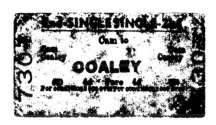

Cam
Date: 1897; Livery: Black, lettered white.

OPC Collection

Cam
Date: 1905; Livery: Black, lettered white.
OPC Collection

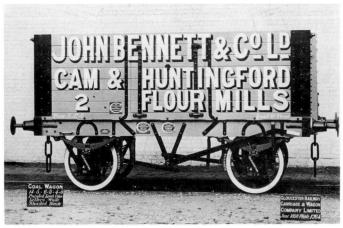

Cam
Date: 1898; Livery: Lead grey, lettered white and shaded black.
OPC Collection

Opened: Goods, 22nd August 1856; Passengers, 18th September 1856
Closed: Passengers, 10th September 1962; Goods, 28th June 1968; As private
siding, 13th July 1970

The terminus of the D&MJR, Dursley, was situated in the bottom of the valley of the River Cam, rather cut off from the town on the hillside. At first the station had a very simple layout, with the engine shed several hundred yards down the line. The station building stood on a short curved platform, opposite which there was a sawmill, served by a siding. The river followed the line along the valley, and it was flanked on both sides by marshy meadows.

The station was altered by the MR around 1890, the station building being extended in a complementary style, and the layout changed to make working easier, introducing a new siding, a dock, and a loading bay. The points were worked from small ground frame huts.

Early in the 20th century, the local firm of R. A. Lister decided to expand their business of making churns and other agricultural equipment, and build a new works on reclaimed marshland around the station. Entering the engineering industry, the works gradually expanded until it stretched down the valley as far as the engine shed. Sidings were laid on both sides of the line, serving the works and its powerhouse, and eventually the station was almost engulfed by the factory. In 1914, a second goods shed was added at the station, reflecting the high level of ordinary goods traffic on the line.

By the 1950s, the station was little used by passengers and had become very shabby . . . in 1962, the passenger service was withdrawn. Ordinary goods trains ceased in 1968, leading to total closure in 1970, the site then being absorbed into Lister's works, all buildings being demolished.

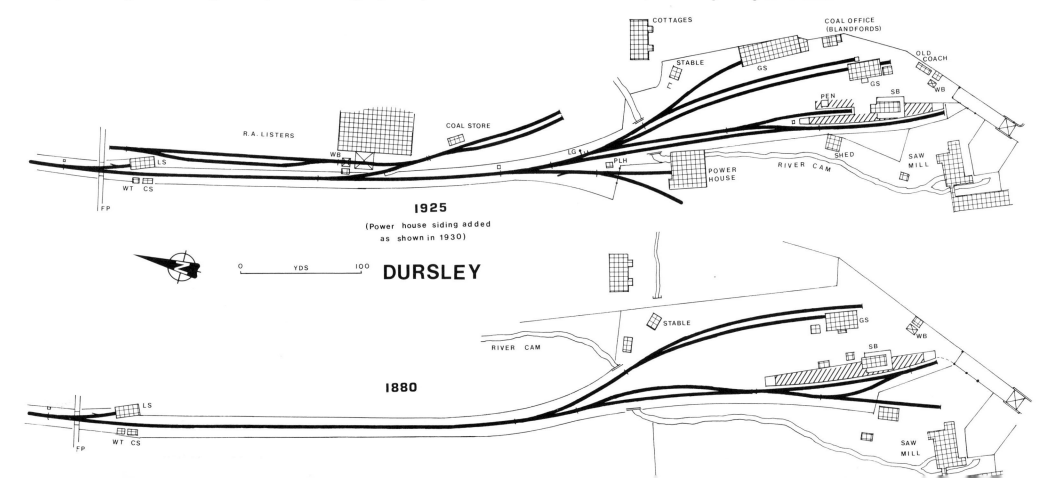

1925
(Power house siding added
as shown in 1930)

DURSLEY

1880

DURSLEY STATION BUILDING

The station building at Dursley was originally a smaller building than that shown in the drawings, although similar in appearance. The building, as first built, resembled a small cottage, with an awning all around, and it had a steeply-pitched slated roof. It was built in red brick, with local stone trimming, and the narrow windows had leaded panes, in the style of Elizabethan buildings.

Around 1890, the building was extended in a complementary style, giving a larger office for the stationmaster, but the symmetry of the structure was lost. This is the building which the drawings show. The gentlemens' toilet was altered by BR in the early 1950s, when the canopy was cut back. The station building was demolished around 1970 to allow for factory extensions on the station site.

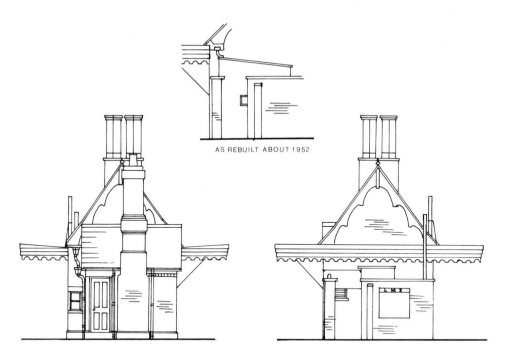

AS REBUILT ABOUT 1952

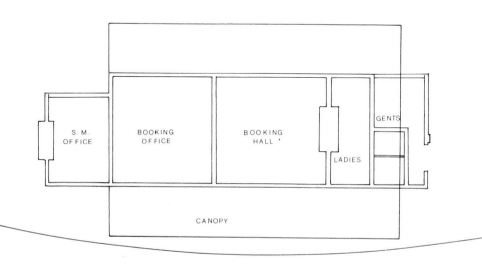

Dursley
Dursley in 1952.

L&GRP

Dursley
The station surrounded by Lister's buildings.

Author's Collection

Dursley
LMS 1F No. 1720 at Dursley in July 1947.

H. C. Casserley

Dursley
Dursley Station in July 1947.

H. C. Casserley

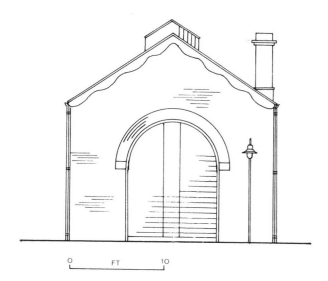

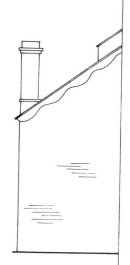

0 FT 10

DURSLEY LOCOMOTIVE SHED

The small engine shed was very unusual in that it was not a purpose-built structure. When the line was being built in 1856, an existing shed was bought for £270 and altered to house the contractor's locomotive. When the line opened, it became the engine shed, being very close to the running line, but some way from the terminus. Locomotives coaled and watered directly from the running line, and there was a small pit on the shed siding. The shed was a brick building, with a slate roof. The entrance was altered, as shown, by the LMS in the 1940s. The shed was closed with the end of passenger traffic, on 18th September 1962, and was soon demolished.

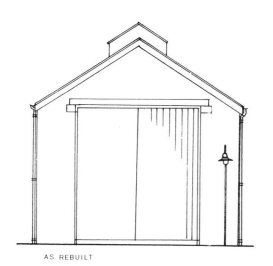

AS REBUILT

Dursley
Dursley engine shed as rebuilt. Ex-LMS 1F No. 41748 takes on water.
Author's Collection

Dursley
Dursley-based private owner wagons.

OPC Collection

Dursley
Dursley in 1947.

H. C. Casserley

Dursley
The station ground frame and yard at Dursley.

H. C. Casserley

SECTION 5

THE THORNBURY BRANCH

The branch line that ran from Yate to Thornbury was authorised in 1864 at the same time as the Mangotsfield to Bath line. Construction began, but the MR was short of money due to the London extension, and had little to spare for branch lines. What there was went to the Bath line, opened in 1869, and the branch did not open throughout until 1872.

Part of the route had actually opened as early as 1868; from Iron Acton, a short branch ran to iron ore quarries near Frampton Cotterell, and this section opened first. Ironically, the deposits were almost worked out, and the line was out of use by 1878, being lifted in 1892. The stub at the junction became a siding.

The other station on the line was Tytherington, and this, together with Iron Acton, had large wooden buildings, similar to that built at Berkeley Road in 1876. There was one platform and no passing loops or goods facilities. The terminus had more substantial buildings to standard MR designs, built in stone. Large stone quarries existed at Tytherington by 1880, providing stone for road building, and these were rail-connected. Trains on the line ran through to Bristol, and had tender engines for the most part, there being a turntable at Thornbury. Class 3F and 4F 0-6-0s were usual in LMS days. The passenger service was hit hard by bus competition, the distance to Bristol being far less by road, and it was withdrawn on 19th April 1944. Goods trains remained, the line finally closing on 3rd September 1967. The track was lifted shortly afterwards.

This was not the end, however, as the building of the M5 motorway close by stimulated the quarries, and it was decided to reopen the line for stone trains. This was done using track lifted from the Bath line, and it reopened on 3rd July 1972, seeming to have a bright future.

Thornbury
An RCTS special at Thornbury in September 1959.

L&GRP

Tytherington
Tytherington Station in 1932. *L&GRP*

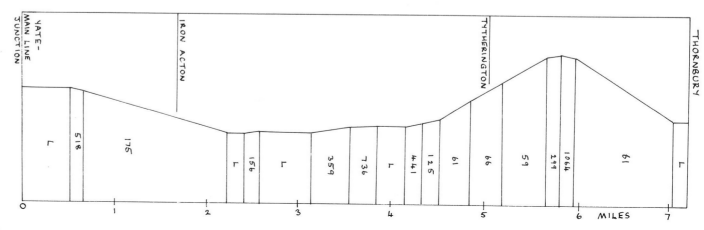

IRON ACTON

Opened: Line to Quarries, 1868; Station, 2nd September 1872
Closed: Passengers, 19th June 1944; Goods, 3rd September 1967

Iron Acton was really a halt, with no goods facilities or sidings other than the old branch, but it had a large wooden building. A signal box existed at the old junction until 1928, the branch having been lifted in 1892 following closure in 1878. The building became derelict, following closure in 1944, and was demolished.

TO IRON ACTON

SP

SB

SP

LC

WB

SC

TO YATE

SP

STREAM

OLD LINE TO FRAMPTON

0   YDS   100

1922

IRON ACTON

Iron Acton
Iron Acton in the 1950s.

C. Maggs

Iron Acton
Iron Acton in the 1960s; the course of the branch to Frampton is on the left.

Lens of Sutton

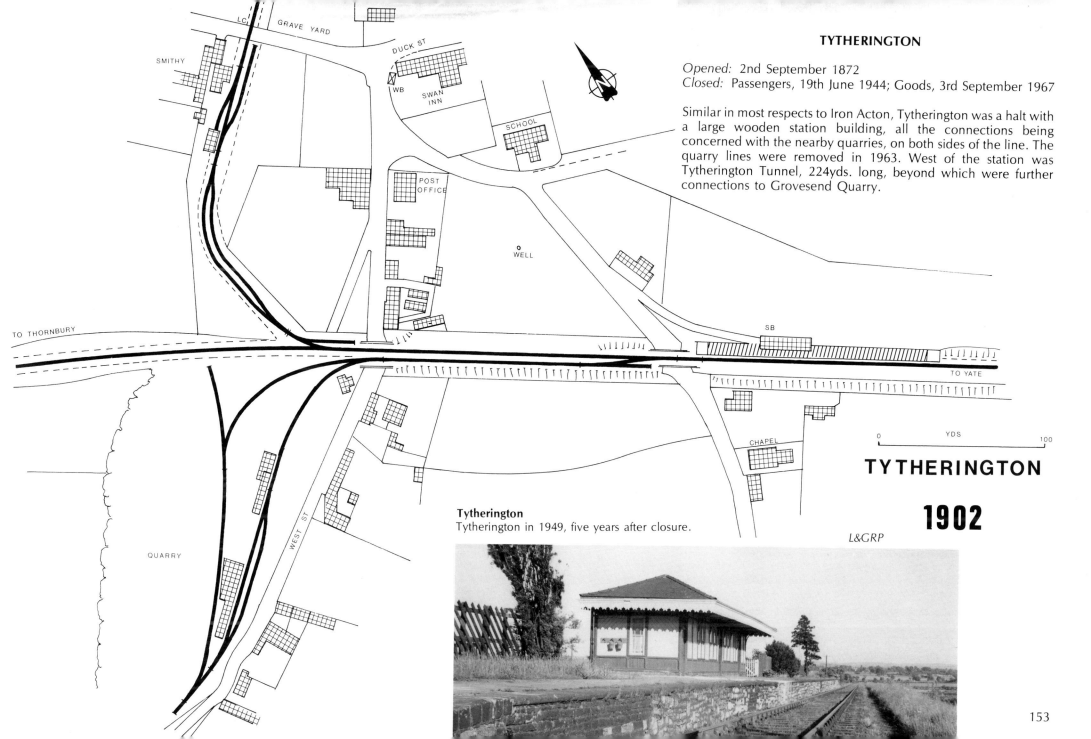

TYTHERINGTON

Opened: 2nd September 1872
Closed: Passengers, 19th June 1944; Goods, 3rd September 1967

Similar in most respects to Iron Acton, Tytherington was a halt with a large wooden station building, all the connections being concerned with the nearby quarries, on both sides of the line. The quarry lines were removed in 1963. West of the station was Tytherington Tunnel, 224yds. long, beyond which were further connections to Grovesend Quarry.

GRAVE YARD

SMITHY

DUCK ST

WB

SWAN INN

SCHOOL

POST OFFICE

○ WELL

SB

TO THORNBURY

TO YATE

CHAPEL

WEST ST

QUARRY

0   YDS   100

TYTHERINGTON

1902

Tytherington
Tytherington in 1949, five years after closure.

L&GRP

153

THORNBURY

Opened: 2nd September 1872
Closed: Passengers, 19th June 1944; Goods, 3rd September 1967

154

Situated 7 miles 31 chains from Yate, Thornbury Station could be considered a 'standard' MR product of the 1870s, the architecture being pure Derby. Most buildings were of grey stone, but the engine shed was a ramshackle wooden affair, coded 8B by the MR. It closed when passenger trains ceased in 1944. The layout of the station was curious, with the cattle pen at the end of the platform road.

The station did not seem to attract photographers when it was open, but fortunately it remained intact until total closure in 1967. The site has now been redeveloped.

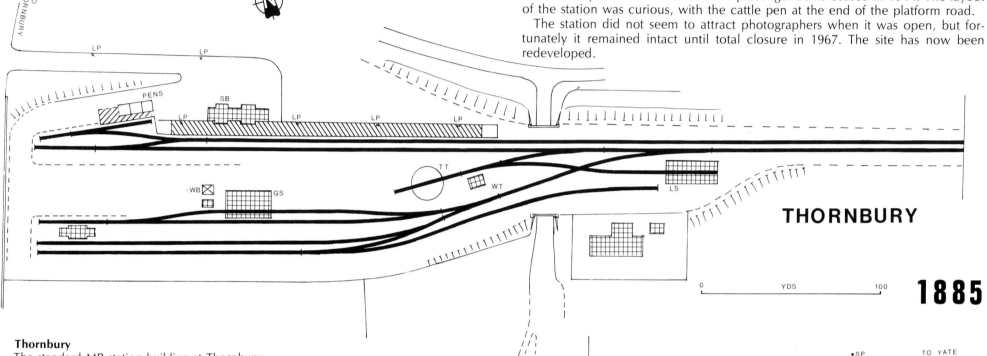

THORNBURY

1885

Thornbury
The standard MR station building at Thornbury.

L&GRP

Thornbury
Thornbury engine shed after closure, showing the station ground frame.
L&GRP

THORNBURY STATION BUILDING

Thornbury was a standard product of the Midland Railway, and the station building was a typical product of the Derby drawing office in the 1870s. Built in local stone, it was of a very attractive design, seen all over the MR system, with minor variations.

This particular example had very ornate bargeboards and ridge tiles, and a tiled roof, which was rather unusual. It lasted long after closure of the station to passengers, but has now been demolished.

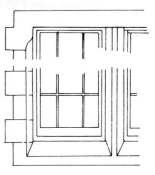

DETAIL OF WINDOW.

DRAIN PIPE (NOT SHOWN)

0   10 FT

BARGE BOARD
NOT SHOWN

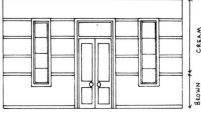

CREAM

BROWN

INTERNAL WALL BEHIND GLASS SCREEN

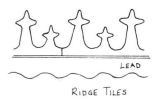

LEAD

RIDGE TILES

DETAIL OF
CHIMNEY

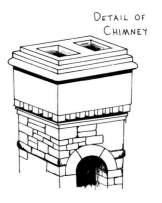

155

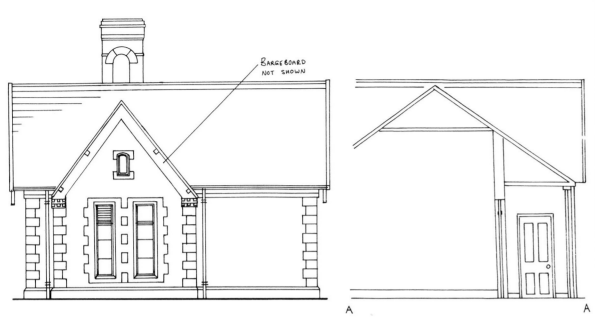

BARGEBOARD
NOT SHOWN

Thornbury
The yard side of the station building at Thornbury.

L&GRP

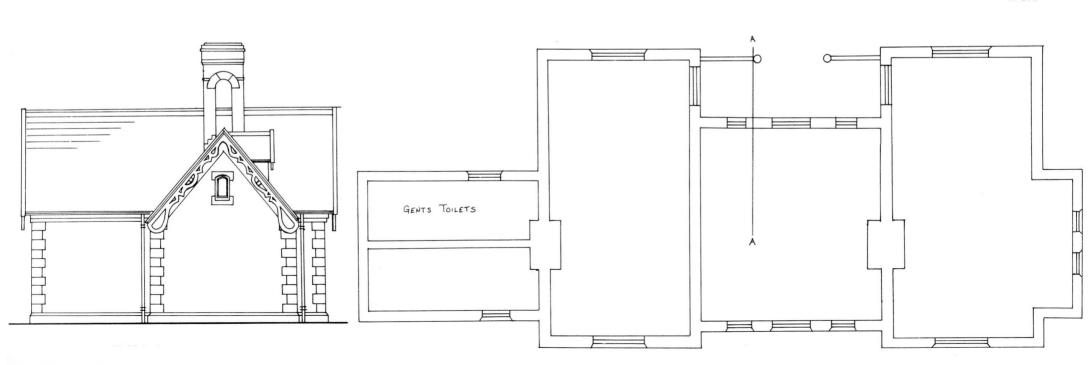

GENTS TOILETS

APPENDIX 1

THE BRISTOL & GLOUCESTER RAILWAY: THE ORIGINAL STATIONS

There were originally six stations on the B&GR, apart from the termini, at Yate, Wickwar, Charfield, Berkeley Road, Frocester and Stonehouse. All opened with the line in 1844, being designed by the line's engineer, I. K. Brunel. He had recently completed the GWR main line, and he designed these stations in a similar manner to the GWR ones. There were, on opening, two very short platforms, which seem to have ended with steps, and a main station building with a matching shelter (except at Wickwar). The buildings were Gothic in design, using brick or stone, with wide wooden canopies, and steeply-pitched slated roofs topped with tall chimneys . . . again Wickwar differed, due to its position.

A square goods shed, with a small lean-to office, and an internal loading platform with a crane and weighing machine, was built at each station, each differing from the others in slight details. The yard side was open. Only at Berkeley Road was a station house provided; a stable was also built here.

The original track layouts were simple. The double track broad gauge main line ran through the platforms, and minimal goods facilities were provided. A plan has survived of Frocester, which shows sidings radiating from a wagon turntable serving the shed, cattle pen, and docks. There was a trailing crossover between the main lines.

The plans of the other stations are conjectural, but I think they are as accurate as possible in the absence of contemporary documents. Yate and Charfield seem to have been similar to Frocester, as shown, Yate having, in addition, a loading bank for iron ore. The facing point may be wrong, but it existed in 1880. Berkeley Road, opened as Dursley & Berkeley, and Stonehouse, seem to have been similar, with the shed on a loop siding; perhaps more traffic was anticipated here. Wickwar was a simpler adaptation of this layout.

These layouts would have remained until 1854, at least, when the gauge was narrowed, although Charfield received a siding serving coal drops in 1846. The MR began to improve the facilities in 1847, building station houses, etc., and the water tower at Charfield. The buildings remained much as built, except for Stonehouse, altered in 1867, although little now remains.

As regards bridges, those now built in brick or stone are original, and those with metal spans were originally wooden, as at Frocester, although the side walls may be original. For further details, see Bibliography.

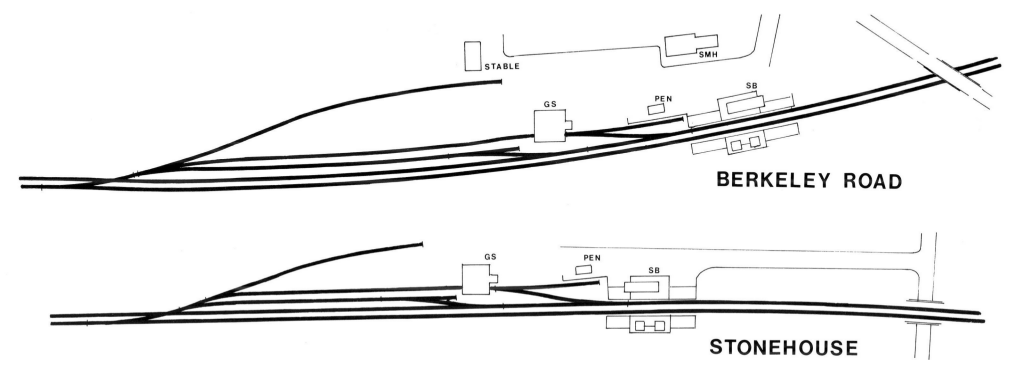

BERKELEY ROAD

STONEHOUSE

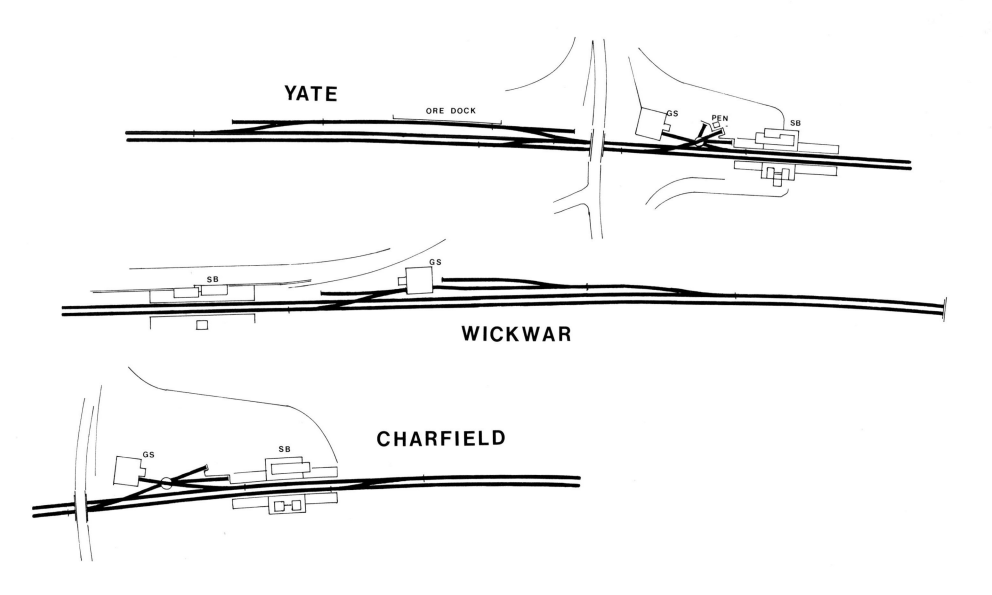

YATE

ORE DOCK

GS   PEN   SB

WICKWAR

SB   GS

CHARFIELD

GS   SB

APPENDIX 2

MIDLAND RAILWAY SIGNALLING IN THE 1870s

It will have become clear to anyone reading this book that the MR lines in Gloucestershire were fully signalled in the 1870s. However, in the course of my researches, I have read several times that the first MR signal box of the familiar wooden type was built in 1882, at London Road Junction, Derby. This is clearly not so, and it may be of interest to consider the evidence of the introduction of signal boxes about 1870, with reference to Gloucestershire in particular.

Small cabins for pointsmen and railway police, of course, existed from the earliest days, and it was a logical step to put all the point and signal levers in one place. Slotted post semaphore signals were introduced on the MR about 1870, with rotating board distant signals, as explained in the HMRS book *Midland Style*. I would suggest that the first cabins would be built at the same time. It is likely that the first cabins would be built at Derby, where their suitability could be easily assessed, but there was certainly a signal box at Shortwood Brickworks Sidings, hardly an important location, in 1872, and at Standish Junction, in 1873.

By 'signal box', I am referring to the direct ancestors of the familiar cabins built all over the MR in the late 1800s; as will be seen, they were very similar indeed, the later cabins being a development of the original design. Most of these early boxes were small, the layouts not being interlocked, and they seem to have been replaced in the 1890s when the new lower quadrant signals were brought into use. Charfield, for instance, had two small signal boxes, which were replaced as late as 1911 by a single larger box.

The evidence for the existence of proper signal boxes in the 1870s is considerable:

(a) Many maps from the period, including Ordnance Survey maps and MR plans, show signal boxes.
(b) Signalling plans from the 1870s exist as reproduced in this book.
(c) A number of photographs taken in the 1870s and 1880s show these boxes, these having been used for the basis of the drawings.

The drawings show a number of variations of the design, which was clearly the forerunner of the more familiar later cabins. The boxes seem to have been small for the most part, many stations having two or more, and some were very tall for sighting reasons. A plan is provided showing the position of a box at Charfield, which must have been tall enough to allow the signalman to see over the road bridge and goods shed. The first drawing shows a box of this type, being only 10ft. square, but very tall. It is likely that access was direct from the road bridge, as shown. Clearly, the height varied according to the location of the box, some being quite squat, but many were far taller than the later replacements.

The second drawing is of a shorter box, 15ft. long x 10ft. wide, while the third shows a large box 30ft. long x 10ft. wide, based on one at Derby. These boxes, like the later ones, were built from a series of prefabricated panels from Derby Works,

thus the dimensions were a combination of the panel lengths. The panels were 10ft. and 15ft. wide, the area above floor level being of constant height; the lower area varied in height to suit the location. All the windows were small and square, arranged in pairs, one pair sliding open in front of the next. On 15ft. panels, the two outer pairs of windows opened. There was no external walkway, and access to the box varied, the door sometimes being in the rear wall. There was no toilet.

The small 10ft. square boxes seem to have been common, while 15ft. x 10ft. boxes were built at such locations as California Crossing, Gloucester. Such places as Tramway Junction had the larger boxes. It is possible to work out quite accurately the size of a box from its shape on a plan. I have yet to find any with a greater width than 10ft.

Livery details were presumably the same as at a later date, and are set out in the HMRS book, *Midland Style*, as are lever colours, etc.

None of these boxes survive in Gloucestershire; the last was Berkeley, closed in 1931, which had an unusual brick base which survives, and which has been measured as a basis for drawings. Elsewhere, there is a similar box at Orton Mere, Nene Valley Railway, on a modern base, and one in use as a store at Appleby.

An enlargement of the photograph of the bridge at Mangotsfield, showing both the original signal box at North Junction and also its replacement, circa 1890. The old box is smaller, probably 10ft. x 10ft., but twice as tall as the new box, which is 20ft. x 10ft. Note also the slotted post signals and the old station house.

National Railway Museum

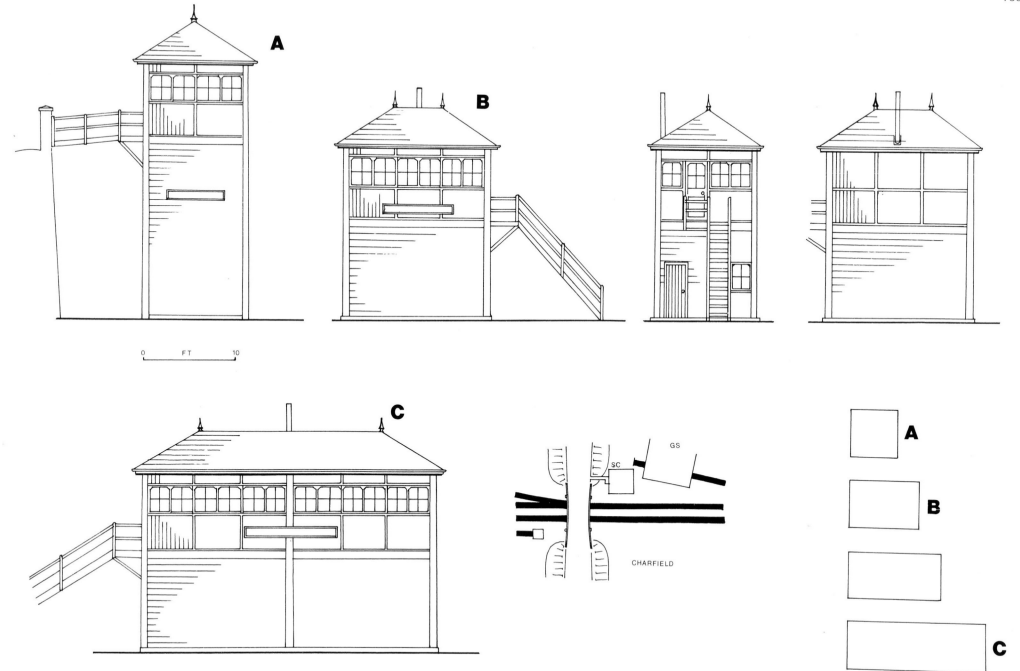

A

B

C

0   FT   10

SC

GS

CHARFIELD

A

B

C